CHESS FUNDAMENTALS

BY JOSÉ R. CAPABLANCA
A PRIMER OF CHESS

CHESS
FUNDAMENTALS

BY

JOSÉ R. CAPABLANCA

CHESS CHAMPION OF THE WORLD

DAVID McKAY COMPANY, INC.
New York

ISBN: 0-679-14004-2

MANUFACTURED IN THE UNITED STATES OF AMERICA

PREFACE

Chess Fundamentals was first published thirteen years ago. Since then there have appeared at different times a number of articles dealing with the so-called Hypermodern Theory. Those who have read the articles may well have thought that something new, of vital importance, had been discovered. The fact is that the Hypermodern Theory is merely the application, during the opening stages generally, of the same old principles through the medium of somewhat new tactics. There has been no change in the fundamentals. The change has been only a change of form, and not always for the best at that.

In chess the tactics may change but the strategic fundamental principles are always the same, so that *Chess Fundamentals* is as good now as it was thirteen years ago. It will be as good a hundred years from now; as long in fact as the laws and rules of the game remain what they are at present. The reader may therefore go over the contents of the book with the assurance that there is in it everything he needs, and that there is nothing to be added and nothing to be changed. *Chess Fundamentals* was the one standard work of its kind thirteen years ago and the author firmly believes that it is the one standard work of its kind now.

J. R. CAPABLANCA

New York
Sept. 1, 1934

LIST OF CONTENTS

PART I

CHAPTER I

FIRST PRINCIPLES: ENDINGS, MIDDLE-GAME AND OPENINGS

CHAPTER II

FURTHER PRINCIPLES IN END-GAME PLAY

CHAPTER III

PLANNING A WIN IN MIDDLE-GAME PLAY

LIST OF CONTENTS

CHAPTER IV

GENERAL THEORY

CHAPTER V

END-GAME STRATEGY

CHAPTER VI

FURTHER OPENINGS AND MIDDLE-GAMES

LIST OF CONTENTS

PART II

ILLUSTRATIVE GAMES

CHESS FUNDAMENTALS

CHESS FUNDAMENTALS

PART I

CHAPTER I

FIRST PRINCIPLES: ENDINGS, MIDDLE-GAME AND OPENINGS

THE first thing a student should do, is to familiarise himself with the power of the pieces. This can best be done by learning how to accomplish quickly some of the simple mates.

1. SOME SIMPLE MATES

Example 1. — The ending Rook and King against King.

The principle is to drive the opposing King to the last line on any side of the board.

In this position the power of the Rook is demonstrated by the first move, R — R 7, which immediately confines the Black King to the last rank, and the mate is quickly accomplished by: 1 R — R 7, K — Kt 1; 2 K — Kt 2.

The combined action of King and Rook is needed to arrive at a position in which mate can be forced. The general principle for a beginner to follow is to

keep his King as much as possible on the same rank, or, as in this case, file, as the opposing King.

When, in this case, the King has been brought to the sixth rank, it is better to place it, not on the same file, but on the one next to it towards the centre.

2...K — B 1; 3 K — B 3, K — K 1; 4 K — K 4, K — Q 1; 5 K — Q 5, K — B 1; 6 K — Q 6.

Not K — B 6, because then the Black King will go back to Q 1 and it will take much longer to mate. If now the King moves back to Q 1, R — R 8 mates at once.

6...K — Kt 1; 7 R — Q B 7, K — R 1; 8 K — B 6, K — Kt 1; 9 K — Kt 6, K — R 1; 10 R — B 8 mate.

It has taken exactly ten moves to mate from the original position. On move 5 Black could have played K — K 1, and, according to principle, White would have continued 6 K — Q 6, K — B 1 (the Black King will ultimately be forced to move in front of the White King and be mated by R — R 8); 7 K — K 6, K — Kt 1; 8 K — B 6, K — R 1; 9 K — Kt 6, K — Kt 1; 10 R — R 8 mate.

Example 2.

Since the Black King is in the centre of the board, the best way to proceed is to advance your own King thus: 1 K — K 2, K — Q 4; 2 K — K 3. As the Rook has not yet come into play, it is better to advance the King straight into the centre of the board, not in front, but to one side of the other King. Should now the Black King move to K 4, the Rook drives it back by R — R 5 ch. On the other hand, if 2... K — B 5 instead, then also 3 R — R 5. If now 3... K — Kt 5, there follows 4 K — Q 3; but if instead 3...K — B 6; then 4 R — R 4, keeping the King confined to as few squares as possible.

Now the ending may continue: 4...K — B 7; 5 R — B 4 ch, K — Kt 6; 6 K — Q 3, K — Kt 7; 7 R — Kt 4 ch, K — R 6; 8 K — B 3, K — R 7. It should be noticed how often the White King has moved next to the Rook, not only to defend it, but also to reduce the mobility of the opposing King. **Now**

White mates in three moves thus: 9 R — R 4 ch, K — Kt 8; 10 R — any square on the Rook's file, forcing the Black King in front of the White, K — B 8; 11 R — R 1 mate. It has taken eleven moves to mate, and, under any conditions, I believe it should be done in under twenty. While it may be monotonous, it is worth while for the beginner to practice such things, as it will teach him the proper handling of his pieces.

Example 3. — Now we come to two Bishops and King against King.

Since the Black King is in the corner, White can play 1 B — Q 3, K — Kt 2; 2 B — K Kt 5, K — B 2; 3 B — B 5, and already the Black King is confined to a few squares. If the Black King, in the original position, had been in the centre of the board, or away from the last row, White should have advanced his King, and then, with the aid of his Bishops, restricted the Black King's movements to as few squares as possible.

We might now continue: 3...K — Kt 2; 4 K — B 2. In this ending the Black King must not only be driven to the edge of the board, but he must also be forced into a corner, and, before a mate can be given, the White King must be brought to the sixth rank and, at the same time, in one of the last two files; in this case either K R 6, K Kt 6, K B 7, K B 8, and as K R 6 and K Kt 6 are the nearest squares, it is to either of these squares that the King ought to go. 4...K — B 2; 5 K — Kt 3, K — Kt 2; 6 K — R 4, K — B 2; 7 K — R 5, K — Kt 2; 8 B — Kt 6, K — Kt 1; 9 K — R 6, K — B 1. White must now mark time and move one of the Bishops, so as to force the Black King to go back; 10 B — R 5, K — Kt 1; 11 B — K 7, K — R 1. Now the White Bishop must take up a position from which it can give check next move along the White diagonal, when the Black King moves back to Kt 1. 12 B — K Kt 4, K — Kt 1; 13 B — K 6 ch, K — R 1; 14 B — B 6 mate.

It has taken fourteen moves to force the mate and, in any position, it should be done in under thirty.

In all endings of this kind, care must be taken not to drift into a stale mate.

In this particular ending one should remember that the King must not only be driven to the edge of the board, but also into a corner. In all such endings, however, it is immaterial whether the King is forced on to the last rank, or to an outside file, e.g. K R 5 or Q R 4, K 1 or Q 8.

Example 4. — We now come to Queen and King against King. As the Queen combines the power of the Rook and the Bishop, it is the easiest mate of all and should always be accomplished in under ten moves. Take the following position:

A good way to begin is to make the first move with the Queen, trying to limit the Black King's mobility as much as possible. Thus: 1 Q — B 6, K — Q 5; 2 K — Q 2. Already the Black King has only one available square 2...K — K 4; 3 K — K 3, K — B 4; 4 Q — Q 6, K — Kt 4. (Should Black play K — Kt 5, then Q — Kt 6 ch); 5 Q — K 6, K — R 5 (if K — R 4, K — B 4 and mate next move); 6 Q — K Kt 6, K — R 6; 7 K — B 3, K moves; 8 Q mates.

In this ending, as in the case of the Rook, the Black King must be forced to the edge of the board; only the Queen being so much more powerful than the Rook, the process is far easier and shorter. These are the three elementary endings and in all of these the principle is the same. In each case the co-operation of the King is needed. In order to force a mate without the aid of the King, at least two Rooks are required.

2. PAWN PROMOTION

The gain of a Pawn is the smallest material advantage that can be obtained in a game ; and it often is sufficient to win, even when the Pawn is the only remaining unit, apart from the Kings. It is essential, speaking generally, that

the King should be in front of his Pawn, with at least one intervening square.

If the opposing King is directly in front of the Pawn, then the game cannot be won. This can best be explained by the following examples.

Example 5.

The position is drawn, and the way to proceed is for Black to keep the King always directly in front of the Pawn, and when it cannot be done, as for instance in this position because of the White King, then the Black King must be kept in front of the White King. The play would proceed thus : 1 P — K 3, K — K 4; 2 K — Q 3, K — Q 4. This is a very important move. Any other move would lose, as will be shown later. As the Black King cannot be kept close up to the Pawn, it must be brought as far forward as possible and, at the same time, in front of the White King.

3 P — K 4 ch, K — K 4; 4 K — K 3, K — K 3; 5 K — B 4, K — B 3. Again the same case. As the White King comes up, the Black King must be kept in front of it, since it cannot be brought up to the Pawn.

6 P — K 5 ch, K — K 3; 7 K — K 4, K – K 2; 8 K — Q 5, K — Q 2; 9 P — K 6 ch, K — K 2; 10 K — K 5, K — K 1; 11 K — Q 6, K — Q 1. If now White advances the Pawn, the Black King gets in front of it and White must either give up the Pawn or play K — K 6, and a stale mate results. If instead of advancing the Pawn White withdraws his King, Black brings his King up to the Pawn and, when forced to go back, he moves to K *in front* of the Pawn ready to come up again or to move in front of the White King, as before, should the latter advance.

The whole mode of procedure is very important and the student should become thoroughly conversant with its details; for it involves principles to be taken up later on, and because many a beginner has lost identical positions from lack of proper knowledge. At this stage of the book I cannot lay too much stress on its importance.

Example 6. — In this position White wins, as the King is in front of his Pawn and there is one intervening square.

The method to follow is to

advance the King as far as is compatible with the safety of the Pawn and never to advance the Pawn until it is essential to its own safety.

Thus:

   1. K — K 4, K — K 3.

Black does not allow the White King to advance, therefore White is now compelled to advance his Pawn so as to force Black to move away. He is then able to advance his own King.

  2. P — K 3, K — B 3; 3. K — Q 5, K — K 2.

If Black had played 3...K — B 4, then White would be forced to advance the Pawn to K 4, since he could not advance his King without leaving Black the opportunity to play K — K 5, winning the Pawn. Since he has not done so, it is better for White not to advance the Pawn yet, since its own safety does not require it, but to try to bring the King still further forward. Thus:

4. K — K 5, K — Q 2;   5. K — B 6, K — K 1.

Now the White Pawn is too far back and it may be brought up within protection of the King.

6. P — K 4, K — Q 2.

Now it would not do to play K — B 7, because Black would play K — Q 3, and White would have to bring back his King to protect the Pawn. Therefore he must continue.

7. P — K 5, K — K 1.

Had he moved anywhere else, White could have played K — B 7, followed by the advance of the Pawn to K 6, K 7, K 8; all these squares being protected by the King. As Black tries to prevent that, White must now force him to move away, at the same time always keeping the King in front of the Pawn. Thus:

8. K — K 6.

P — K 6 would make it a draw, as Black would then play K — B, and we would have a position similar to the one explained in connection with Example 5.

8...K — B 1;   9 K — Q 7.

King moves and the White Pawn advances to K 8, becomes a Queen, and it is all over.

This ending is like the previous one, and for the same reasons should be thoroughly understood before proceeding any further.

3. PAWN ENDINGS

I shall now give a couple of simple endings of two Pawns against one, or three against two, that the reader may see how they can be won. Fewer explanations will be given, as it is up to the student to work things out for himself. Furthermore, nobody can learn how to play well merely from the study of a book; it can only serve as a guide and the rest must be done by the teacher, if the student has one; if not, the student must realise by long and bitter experience the practical application of the many things explained in the book.

Example 7.

In this position White cannot win by playing
1 P — B 6, because Black plays, not P × P, which
would lose, but 1...K — Kt 1, and if then 2 P × P,
K × P, and draws, as shown in a previous case. If
2 P — B 7 ch, K — B 1, and White will never be
able to Queen his Pawn without losing it. If
2 K — K 7, P × P; 3 K × P, K — B 1, and draws.
White, however, can win the position given in the
diagram by playing:

1 K — Q 7, K — Kt 1; 2 K — K 7, K — R 1;
3 P — B 6, P × P. If 3...K — Kt 1; 4 P — B 7 ch,
K — R 1; 5 P — B 8 (Q) mate.

4 K — B 7, P — B 4; 5 P — Kt 7 ch, K — R 2;
6 P — Kt 8 (Q) ch, K — R 3; 7 Q — Kt 6 mate.

Example 8. — In the above position White can't win
by 1 P — B 5. Black's best answer would be P — Kt 3
draws. (The student should work this out.) He
cannot win by 1 P — Kt 5, because P — Kt 3 draws.
(This, because of the principle of the *"opposition"*

which governs this ending as well as all the Pawn-endings already given, and which will be explained more fully later on.)

White can win, however, by playing: 1 K — K 4, K — K 3. (If 1...P — Kt 3; 2 K — Q 4, K — K 3; 3 K — B 5, K — B 3; 4 K — Q 6, K — B 2; 5 P — Kt 5, K — Kt 2; 6 K — K 7, K — Kt 1; 7 K — B 6, K — R 2; 8 K — B 7 and White wins the Pawn.)

2 P — B 5 ch, K — B 3; 3 K — B 4, P — Kt 3. (If this Pawn is kept back we arrive at the ending shown in Example 7.) 4 P — Kt 5 ch, K — B 2; 5 P — B 6, K — K 3; 6 K — K 4, K — B 2; 7 K — K 5, K — B 1. White cannot force his Bishop's Pawn into Q (find out why), but by giving his Pawn up he can win the other Pawn and the game. Thus:

8 P — B 7, K × P; 9 K — Q 6, K — B 1; 10 K — K 6, K — Kt 2; 11 K — K 7, K — Kt 1; 12 K — B 6, K — R 2; 13 K — B 7, K — R 1; 14 K × P, K — Kt 1.

There is still some resistance in Black's position. In fact, the only way to win is the one given here, as will easily be seen by experiment.

15 K — R 6 (if K — B 6, K — R 2; and in order to win White must get back to the actual position, as against 16 P — Kt 6 ch, K — R 1 draws), K — R 1; 16 P — Kt 6, K — Kt 1; 17 P — Kt 7, K — B 2; 18 K — R 7, and White queens the Pawn and wins.

This ending, apparently so simple, should show the student the enormous difficulties to be surmounted, even when there are hardly any pieces left, when playing against an adversary who knows how to use the resources at his disposal, and it should show the student, also, the necessity of paying strict attention to these elementary things which form the basis of true mastership in Chess.

Example 9. — In this ending

White can win by advancing any of the three Pawns on the first move, but it is convenient to follow the general rule, whenever there is no good reason against it, of *advancing the Pawn that has no Pawn opposing it*. Thus we begin by —

1. P — B 5, K — K 2.

If P — Kt 3, P — B 6; and we have a similar ending to one of those shown above. If 1...P — R 3; 2 P — Kt 5.

2. K — K 5, K — B 2; 3. P — Kt 5, K — K 2.

If 3...P — Kt 3; 4 P — B 6, and if 3...P — R 3; 4 P — Kt 6 ch, and in either case we have a similar ending to one of those already shown.

4. P — R 5,

and by following it up with P — Kt 6 we have the same ending previously shown. Should Black play 4...P — Kt 3, then R P × P, P × P; P — B 6 ch with the same result.

Having now seen the cases when the Pawns are all on one side of the board we shall now examine a case when there are Pawns on both sides of the board.

Example 10. — In these cases the general rule is to *act immediately on the side where you have the su-*

perior forces. Thus we have:

1. P — K Kt 4.

It is generally advisable to advance the Pawn that is free from opposition.

1. .... P — Q R 4.

Black makes an advance on the other side, and now White considers whether or not he should stop the advance. In this case either way wins, but generally the advance should be stopped when the opposing King is far away.

2. P — Q R 4, K — B 3; 3. P — R 4, K — K 3.

If 3...K — Kt 3, then simple counting will show that White goes to the other side with his King, wins the P at Q R 4, and then Queens his single Pawn long before Black can do the same.

4. P — Kt 5, K — B 2; 5. K — B 5, K — Kt 2; 6. P — R 5, K — B 2.

If 6...P — R 3; 7 P — Kt 6, and then the two Pawns defend themselves and White can go to the other side with his King, to win the other Pawn.

7. K — K 5.

Now it is time to go to the other side with the King, win the Black Pawn and Queen the single Pawn. This is typical of all such endings and should be worked out by the student in this case and in similar cases which he can put up.

4. SOME WINNING POSITIONS IN THE MIDDLE-GAME

By the time the student has digested all that has been previously explained, he, no doubt, is anxious to get to the actual game and play with all the pieces. However, before considering the openings, we shall devote a little time to some combinations that often arise during the game, and which will give the reader some idea of the beauty of the game, once he becomes better acquainted with it.

Example 11.

It is Black's move, and thinking that White merely threatens to play Q — R 6 and to mate at K Kt 7, Black plays 1...R — K 1, threatening mate by way of R — K 8. White now uncovers his real and most effective threat, viz.:

1...R — K 1; 2 Q × P ch, K × Q; 3 R — R 3 ch, K — Kt 1; 4 R — R 8 mate.

This same type of combination may come as the result of a somewhat more complicated position.

Example 12.

White is a piece behind, and unless he can win it back quickly he will lose; he therefore plays:

　　1. Kt × Kt　　　　B — Kt 4

He cannot take the Kt because White threatens mate by Q × P ch followed by R — R 3 ch.

　　2. Kt — K 7 ch　　　Q × Kt

Again if B × Kt; Q × P ch, K × Q; R — R 3 ch, King moves; R — R 8 mate.

　　3. R × Q　　　　　B × R
　　4. Q — Q 7

and White wins one of the two Bishops, remains with a Q and a B against a R and B, and should therefore win easily. These two examples show the danger of advancing the K Kt P one square, after having Castled on that side.

Example 13.

This is another very interesting type of combination. Black has a R for a Kt and should therefore win, unless White is able to obtain some compensation immediately. White, in fact, mates in a few moves thus:

      1. Kt — B 6 ch   P × Kt

Forced, otherwise Q × P mates.

      2. Q — Kt 3 ch   K — R 1

      3. B × P mate.

Example 14. — The same type of combination occurs in a more complicated form in the following position.

1. B × Kt		Q × B.

If...B × Kt; Q — B 3 threatens mate, and therefore wins the Q, which is already attacked.

2. Kt — B 6 ch		P × Kt
3. R — Kt 3 ch		K — R 1
4. B × P mate.		

Example 15. — A very frequent type of combination is shown in the following position.

Here White is the exchange and a Pawn behind, but he can win quickly thus: 1 B × P ch, K × B. (If 1...K — R 1; 2 Q — K R 5, P — K Kt 3; 3 Q — R 6, and wins.)

2 Q — R 5 ch, K — Kt 1; 3 Kt — Kt 5, and Black cannot stop mate at K R 7 except by sacrificing the Queen by Q — K 5, which would leave White with a Q for a R.

Example 16. — This same type of combination is seen in a more complicated form in the following position.

White proceeds as follows: 1 Kt × Kt ch (this clears the line for the B); B × Kt (to stop the Kt from moving to Kt 5 after the sacrifice of the B); 2 R × B, Kt × R best; 3 B × P ch, K × B. (If 3...K — R 1; 4 Q — R 5, P — K Kt 3; 5 B × P ch, K — Kt 2; 6 Q — R 7 ch, K — B 3; 7 P — Kt 5 ch, K — K 3; 8 B × P ch, R × B; 9 Q — K 4 mate.) 4 Q — R 5 ch, K — Kt 1; 5 Kt — Kt 5, R — B 1;

6 Q—R 7 ch, K—B 1; 7 Q—R 8 ch, Kt—Kt 1; 8 Kt—R 7 ch, K—K 2; 9 R—K 1 ch, K—Q 1; 10 Q × Kt mate.

This combination is rather long and has many variations, therefore a beginner will hardly be able to fathom it; but, knowing the type of combination, he might under similar circumstances undertake and carry out a brilliant attack which he would otherwise never think of. It will be seen that all the combinations shown have for a foundation the proper co-ordination of the pieces, which have all been brought to bear against a weak point.

5. RELATIVE VALUE OF THE PIECES

Before going on to the general principles of the openings, it is advisable to give the student an idea of the proper relative value of the pieces. There is no complete and accurate table for all of them, and the only thing to do is to compare the pieces separately.

For all general theoretical purposes the Bishop and the Knight have to be considered as of the same value, though it is my opinion that the Bishop will prove the more valuable piece in most cases; and it is well known that two Bishops are almost always better than two Knights.

The Bishop will be stronger against Pawns than the Knight, and in combination with Pawns will also be stronger against the Rook than the Knight will be.

A Bishop and a Rook are also stronger than a Knight and a Rook, but a Queen and a Knight may be stronger than a Queen and a Bishop.

A Bishop will often be worth more than three Pawns, but a Knight very seldom so, and may even not be worth so much.

A Rook will be worth a Knight and two Pawns, or a Bishop and two Pawns, but, as said before, the Bishop will be a better piece against the Rook.

Two Rooks are slightly stronger than a Queen. They are slightly weaker than two Knights and a Bishop, and a little more so than two Bishops and a Knight. The power of the Knight decreases as the pieces are changed off. The power of the Rook, on the contrary, increases.

The King, a purely *defensive* piece throughout the middle-game, becomes an *offensive* piece once all the pieces are off the board, and sometimes even when there are one or two minor pieces left. The handling of the King becomes of paramount importance once the end-game stage is reached.

6. GENERAL STRATEGY OF THE OPENING

The main thing is to *develop the pieces quickly*. Get them into play as fast as you can.

From the outset two moves, 1 P — K 4 or 1 P — Q 4, open up lines for the Queen and a Bishop. Therefore, theoretically one of these two moves must be the best, as no other first move accomplishes so much.

Example 17. — Suppose we begin :

  1. P — K 4   P — K 4
  2. Kt — K B 3

This is both an attacking and a developing move. Black can now either reply with the identical move or play

  2. ....   Kt — Q B 3

This developing move at the same time defends the King's Pawn.

  3. Kt — B 3   Kt — B 3

These moves are of a purely developing nature.

    4. B — Kt 5

It is generally advisable not to bring this Bishop out until one Knight is out, preferably the King's Knight. The Bishop could also have been played to B 4, but it is advisable whenever possible to combine development and attack.

  4. ....   B — Kt 5

Black replies in the same manner, threatening a possible exchange of Bishop for Knight with Kt × P to follow.

    5. O — O

an indirect way of preventing 5...B × Kt, which more experience or study will show to be bad. At the same time *the Rook is brought into action in the centre, a very important point.*

5. ....   O — O

Black follows the same line of reasoning.

6. P — Q 3   P — Q 3

These moves have a two-fold object, viz.: to protect the King's Pawn and to open the diagonal for the development of the Queen's Bishop.

7. B — Kt 5

A very powerful move, which brings us to the middle-game stage, as there is already in view a combination to win quickly by Kt — Q 5. This threat makes it impossible for Black to continue the same course. (There is a long analysis showing that Black should lose if he also plays B — Kt 5.) He is now forced to play 7...B × Kt, as experience has shown, thus bringing up to notice three things.

First, the complete development of the opening has taken only seven moves. (This varies up to ten or twelve moves in some very exceptional cases. As a rule, eight should be enough.) Second, Black has been compelled to exchange a Bishop for a Knight, but as a compensation he has isolated White's Q R P and doubled a Pawn. (This, at such an early stage of the game, is rather an advantage for White, as the Pawn is doubled towards the centre of the board.) Third, White by the exchange brings up a Pawn to control the square Q 4, puts Black on the defensive, as experience will show, and thus keeps *the initiative*, an unquestionable advantage.[1]

The strategical principles expounded above are the same for all the openings, only their tactical application varies according to the circumstances.

Before proceeding further I wish to lay stress on the following point which the student should bear in mind.

Before development has been completed no piece should be moved more than once, unless it is essential in order to obtain either material advantage or to secure freedom of action.

The beginner would do well to remember this, as well as what has already been stated: viz., *bring out the Knights before bringing out the Bishops.*

7. CONTROL OF THE CENTRE

The four squares, K 4 and Q 4 on each side respectively, are the centre squares, and control of these squares is called control of the centre. *The control of the centre is of great importance.* No violent attack can succeed without controlling at least two of these

[1] The value of the initiative is explained in section 20, p. 77.

squares, and possibly three. Many a manœuvre in the opening has for its sole object the control of the centre, which invariably ensures the initiative. It is well always to bear this in mind, since it will often be the reason of a series of moves which could not otherwise be properly understood. As this book progresses I shall dwell more fully on these different points. At present I shall devote some time to openings taken at random and explain the moves according to general principles. The student will in that way train his mind in the proper direction, and will thus have less trouble in finding a way out when confronted with a new and difficult situation.

Example 18.

1.	P — K 4	P — K 4
2.	Kt — K B 3	P — Q 3

A timid move. Black assumes a defensive attitude at once. On principle the move is wrong. In the openings, whenever possible, *pieces should be moved in preference to Pawns*.

3.	P — Q 4

White takes the offensive immediately and strives to control the centre so as to have ample room to deploy his forces.

3.	....	Kt — Q 2

Black does not wish to relinquish the centre and also prefers the text move to Kt — Q B 3, which would be the more natural square for the Kt. But on prin-

ciple the move is wrong, because it blocks the action
of the Queen's Bishop, and instead of facilitating the
action of Black's pieces, tends, on the contrary, to
cramp them.

4. B — Q B 4   P — K R 3

Black is forced to pay the penalty of his previous
move. Such a move on Black's part condemns by
itself any form of opening that makes it necessary.
White threatened Kt — Kt 5 and Black could not stop
it with 4...B — K 2, because of 5 P × P, Kt × P
(if 5...P × P, 6 Q — Q 5); 6 Kt × Kt, P × Kt;
7 Q — R 5, and White wins a Pawn and has besides a
perfectly safe position.

5. Kt — B 3   K Kt — B 3
6. B — K 3   B — K 2
7. Q — K 2

It should be noticed that White does not Castle yet.
The reason is that he wants to deploy his forces first,
and through the last move force Black to play
P — Q B 3 to make room for the Queen as White
threatens R — Q 1, to be followed by P × P. Black's
other alternatives would finally force him to play
P × P, thus abandoning the centre to White.

7. ....   P — B 3
8. R — Q 1   Q — B 2
9. O – O

With this last move White completes his development,
while Black is evidently somewhat hampered. A simple
examination will suffice to show that White's position

is unassailable. There are no weak spots in his armour, and his pieces are ready for any manœuvre that he may wish to carry out in order to begin the attack on the enemy's position. The student should carefully study this example. It will show him that it is sometimes convenient to delay Castling. I have given the moves as they come to my mind without following any standard book on openings. Whether the moves given by me agree or not with the standard works, I do not know, but at the present stage of this book it is not convenient to enter into discussions of mere technicalities which the student will be able to understand when he has become more proficient.

Example 19.

1.	P — K 4	P — K 4
2.	Kt — K B 3	P — Q 3
3.	P — Q 4	B — Kt 5

A bad move, which violates one of the principles set down, according to which at least one Knight should be developed before the Bishops are brought out, and also because it exchanges a Bishop for a Knight, which in the opening is generally bad, unless there is some compensation.

4.	P × P	B × Kt

4...P × P loses a Pawn.

5.	Q × B	P × P
6.	B — Q B 4	Q — B 3

If Kt — B 3 ; Q — Q Kt 3 wins a Pawn.

    7. Q — Q Kt 3   P — Q Kt 3
    8. Kt — B 3   P — Q B 3

To prevent Kt — Q 5.

Black, however, has no pieces out except his Queen, and White, with a Bishop and a Knight already developed, has a chance of obtaining an advantage quickly by playing Kt — Q 5 anyway. The student is left to work out the many variations arising from this position.

These examples will show the practical application of the principles previously enunciated. The student is warned against playing Pawns in preference to pieces at the beginning of the game, especially P — K R 3 and P — Q R 3, which are moves very commonly indulged in by beginners.

8. TRAPS

I shall now give a few positions or traps to be avoided in the openings, and in which (practice has shown) beginners are often caught.

Example 20.

White plays:

   1. P × P   Kt × P

Black should have recaptured with the **Pawn.**

   2. Kt   Kt   B × Q
   3. B × P ch   K — K 2
   4. Kt — Q 5 mate.

Example 21.

Black, having the move, should play P — K 3. But
suppose he plays Kt — K B 3 instead, then comes —

      1. B × P ch

Kt — K 5 would also give White the advantage, the
threat being of course if B × Q; 2 B × P mate. Nor
does B — R 5 help matters, because of 2 Q × B, 1 . . .
B — K 3 leaves Black with the inferior position. But
White's move in the text secures an immediate material
advantage, and the beginner at any rate should never
miss such an opportunity for the sake of a speculative
advantage in position.

      1. . . . .   K × B
      2. Kt — K 5 ch   K moves
      3. Kt × B

and White has won a Pawn besides having the better
position.

    There are a good many other traps — in fact, there
is a book written on traps on the chess board; but
the type given above is the most common of all.

CHAPTER II

FURTHER PRINCIPLES IN END-GAME PLAY

WE shall now go back to the endings in search of a few more principles, then again to the middle-game, and finally to the openings once more, so that the advance may not only be gradual but homogeneous. In this way the foundation on which we expect to build the structure will be firm and solid.

9. A CARDINAL PRINCIPLE

In the position shown above, White can draw by playing P — Kt 4 according to the general rule that governs such cases, i.e. *to advance the Pawn that is free from opposition*. But suppose that White, either because he does not know this principle or because he does not, in this case, sufficiently appreciate the value of its application; suppose, we say, that he plays 1 P — Q R 4. Then Black can win by playing 1... P — Q R 4, applying one of the cardinal principles of the high strategy of chess —

A unit that holds two.

In this case one Pawn would hold two of the opponent's Pawns. The student cannot lay too much stress on this principle. It can be applied in many ways, and it constitutes one of the principal weapons in the hands of a master.

Example 22. — The example given should be sufficient proof. We give a few moves of the main variation: —

1.	P — R 4	P — Q R 4
2.	K — Kt 2	K — B 5
	(Best; see why.)	
3.	P — Kt 4	P × P
	(Best.)	
4.	P — R 5	P — Kt 6
5.	P — R 6	P — Kt 7
6.	P — R 7	P — Kt 8 (Q)
7.	P — R 8 (Q)	Q — K 5 ch
8.	Q × Q	K × Q

This brings the game to a position which is won by Black, and which constitutes one of the classical endings of King and Pawns. I shall try to explain the guiding idea of it to those not familiar with it.

10. A CLASSICAL ENDING

Example 23. — In this position White's best line of defence consists in keeping his Pawn where it stands at R 2. As soon as the Pawn is advanced it becomes easier for Black to win. On the other hand, Black's plan to win (supposing that White does not advance his Pawn) may be divided into three parts. The first part will be to get his King to K R 6, at the same time keeping intact the position of his Pawns. (This is all important, since, in order to win the game, it is essential at the end that Black may be able to advance his rearmost Pawn one or two squares according to the position of the White King.)

1. K — Kt 3   K — K 6
2. K — Kt 2

If 2 K — Kt 4, K — B 7; 3 P — R 4, P — Kt 3 will win.

2. ....   K — B 5
3. K — B 2   K — Kt 5
4. K — Kt 2   K — R 5
5. K — Kt 1   K — R 6

The first part has been completed.

The second part will be short and will consist in advancing the R P up the K.

6. K — R 1   P — R 4
7. K — Kt 1   P — R 5

This ends the second part.

The third part will consist in timing the advance of the Kt P so as to play P — Kt 6 when the White King is at R 1. It now becomes evident how necessary it is to be able to move the Kt P either one or two squares according to the position of the White King, as indicated previously.[1] In this case, as it is White's move, the Pawn will be advanced two squares since the White King will be in the corner, but if it were now Black's move the Kt P should only be advanced one square since the White King is at Kt 1.

8.	K — R 1	P — Kt 4
9.	K — Kt 1	P — KT 5
10.	K — R 1	P — Kt 6
11.	P × P	

If K — Kt 1, P — Kt 7.

11.	. . . .	P × P
12.	K — Kt 1	P — Kt 7
13.	K — B 2	K — R 7

and wins.

It is in this analytical way that the student should try to learn. He will thus train his mind to follow a logical sequence in reasoning out any position. This example is excellent training, since it is easy to divide it into three stages and to explain the main point of each part.

The next subject we shall study is the simple oppo-

[1] See page 37.

sition, but before we devote our time to it I wish to call attention to two things.

11. OBTAINING A PASSED PAWN

When three or more Pawns are opposed to each other in some such position as the one in Example 24, there is always a chance for one side or the other of obtaining a passed Pawn.

Example 24. — In the above position the way of obtaining a passed Pawn is to advance the centre Pawn.

1.	P — Kt 6	R P × P

If B P × P; P — R 6,

2.	P — B 6	P × B P
3.	P — R 6	

and as in this case the White Pawn is nearer to Queen than any of the Black Pawns, White will

win. Now if it had been Black's move Black could play

1.	P — Kt 3
2. B P × P	B P × P

It would not be advisable to try to obtain a passed Pawn because the White Pawns would be nearer to Queen than the single Black Pawn.

3. P × P	P × P

and the game properly played would be a draw. The student should work this out for himself.

12. HOW TO FIND OUT WHICH PAWN WILL BE FIRST TO QUEEN

When two Pawns are free, or will be free, to advance to Queen, you can find out, by counting, which Pawn will be the first to succeed.

Example 25. — In this position whoever moves first wins.

The first thing is to find out, by counting, whether the opposing King can be in time to stop the passed Pawn from Queening. When, as in this case, it cannot be done, the point is to count which Pawn comes in first. In this case the time is the same, but the Pawn that reaches the eighth square first and becomes a Queen is in a position to capture the adversary's Queen when he makes one. Thus:

1.	P — R 4	P — K R 4
2.	P — R 5	P — R 5
3.	P — Kt 6	P × P

Now comes a little calculation. White can capture the Pawn, but if he does so, he will not, when Queening, command the square where Black will also Queen his Pawn. Therefore, instead of taking, he plays:

4.	P — R 6	P — R 6
5.	P — R 7	P — R 7
6.	P — R 8 (Q), and wins.	

The student would do well to acquaint himself with various simple endings of this sort, so as to acquire the habit of counting, and thus be able to know with ease when he can or cannot get there first. Once again I must call attention to the fact that a book cannot by itself teach how to play. It can only serve as a guide, and the rest must be learned by experience, and if a teacher can be had at the same time, so much the faster will the student be able to learn.

13. THE OPPOSITION

When Kings have to be moved, and one player can, by force, bring his King into a position similar to the one shown in the following diagram, so that his adversary is forced to move and make way for him, the player obtaining that advantage is said to have *the opposition.*

Example 26. — Suppose in the above position White plays

1. K — Q 4

Now Black has the option of either opposing the passage of the White King by playing K — Q 3 or, if he prefers, he can *pass* with his own King by replying K — B 4. Notice that the Kings are directly opposed to each other, and the number of intervening squares between them is odd — one in this case.

The opposition can take the form shown above,

which can be called actual or close frontal opposition;
or this form:

which can be called actual or close diagonal opposition.
or, again, this form:

which can be called actual or close lateral opposition.

In practice they are all one and the same. The Kings are always on squares of the same colour, there is only one intervening square between the Kings, and the player who has moved last "*has the opposition.*"

Now, if the student will take the trouble of moving each King backwards as in a game in the same frontal, diagonal or lateral line respectively shown in the diagrams, we shall have what may be called *distant* frontal, diagonal and lateral opposition respectively.

The matter of the opposition is highly important, and takes at times somewhat complicated forms, all of which can be solved mathematically; but, for the present, the student should only consider the most simple forms. (An examination of some of the examples of King and Pawns endings already given will show several cases of close opposition.)

In all simple forms of opposition,
when the Kings are on the same line and the number of intervening squares between them is even, the player who has the move has the opposition.

Example 27. — The above position shows to advantage the enormous value of the opposition. The

position is very simple. Very little is left on the board, and the position, to a beginner, probably looks absolutely even. It is not the case, however. *Whoever has the move wins*. Notice that the Kings are directly in front of one another, and that the number of intervening squares is *even*.

Now as to the procedure to win such a position. The proper way to begin is to move straight up. Thus:

1.	K — K 2	K — K 2
2.	K — K 3	K — K 3
3.	K — K 4	K — B 3

Now White can exercise the option of either playing K — Q 5 and thus passing with his King, or of playing K — B 4 and prevent the Black King from passing, thereby keeping the opposition. Mere counting will show that the former course will only lead to a draw, therefore White takes the latter course and plays:

4.	K — B 4	K — Kt 3

If 4...K — K 3; 5 K — Kt 5 will win.

5.	K — K 5	K — Kt 2

Now by counting it will be seen that White wins by capturing Black's Knight Pawn.

The process has been comparatively simple in the variation given above, but Black has other lines of defence more difficult to overcome. Let us begin anew.

1. K — K 2   K — Q 1

Now if 2 K — Q 3, K — Q 2, or if 2 K — K 3, K — K 2, and Black obtains the opposition in both cases. (When the Kings are directly in front of one another, and the number of intervening squares between the Kings is *odd*, the player who has moved last has the opposition.)

Now in order to win, the White King must advance. There is only one other square where he can go, B 3, and that is the right place. Therefore it is seen that in such cases when the opponent makes a so-called waiting move, you must advance, leaving a rank or file free between the Kings. Therefore we have —

2. K — B 3   K — K 2

Now, it would be bad to advance, because then Black, by bringing up his King in front of your King, would obtain the opposition. It is White's turn to play a similar move to Black's first move, viz. :

3. K — K 3

which brings the position back to the first variation shown. The student would do well to familiarise himself with the handling of the King in all examples of opposition. It often means the winning or losing of a game.

Example 28. — The following position is an excellent proof of the value of the opposition as a means of defence.

White is a Pawn behind and apparently lost, yet he can manage to draw as follows:

1. K — R 1 !

The position of the Pawns does not permit White to draw by means of the actual or close opposition, hence he takes the distant opposition: in effect if 1 K — B 1 (actual or close opposition), K — Q 7; 2 K — B 2, K — Q 6 and White cannot continue to keep the lateral opposition essential to his safety, because of his own Pawn at B 3. On the other hand, after the text move, if

1.	K — Q 7
2. K — R 2	K — Q 6
3. K — R 3 !	K — K 7

4. K — Kt 2	K — K 6
5. K — Kt 3	K — Q 5
6. K — Kt 4	

attacking the Pawn and forcing Black to play 6...
K — K 6 when he can go back to Kt 3 as already
shown, and always keep the opposition.

Going back to the original position, if

| 1. K — R 1 | P — Kt 5 |

White does not play P × P, because P — K 5 will
win, but plays:

| 2. K — Kt 2 | K — Q 7 |

If 2...P × P ch; 3 K × P, followed by K — K 4,
will draw.

| 3. P × P | P — K 5 |

and mere counting will show that both sides Queen,
drawing the game.

If the student will now take the trouble to go back
to the examples of King and Pawns which I have
given in this book,[1] he will realise that in all of them
the matter of the opposition is of paramount importance; as, in fact, it is in nearly all endings of King
and Pawns, except in such cases where the Pawn-
position in itself ensures the win.

[1] See page 13.

14. THE RELATIVE VALUE OF KNIGHT AND BISHOP

Before turning our attention to this matter it is well to state now that *two Knights alone cannot mate,* but, under certain conditions of course, they can do so if the opponent has one or more Pawns.

Example 29. — In the above position White cannot win, although the Black King is cornered, but in the following position, in which Black has a Pawn,

White wins with or without the move. **Thus:**

    1. Kt — Kt 6   P — R 5

White cannot take the Pawn because the game will be drawn, as explained before.

2.	Kt — K 5	P — R 6
3.	Kt — B 6	P — R 7
4.	Kt — Kt 5	P — R 8 (Q)
5.	Kt — B 7 mate	

The reason for this peculiarity in chess is eviaent. *White with the two Knights can only stalemate the King, unless Black has a Pawn which can be moved.*

Example 30. —Although he is a Bishop and a Pawn ahead the following position cannot be won by White.

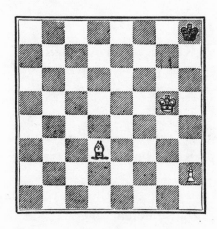

It is the greatest weakness of the Bishop, that when the Rook's Pawn Queens on a square of opposite colour and the opposing King is in front of the Pawn, the Bishop is absolutely worthless. All that Black has to do is to keep moving his King close to the corner square.

Example 31. — In the above position White with or without the move can win. Take the most difficult variation.

1.	....	K — R 7
2.	Kt — Kt 4 ch	K — R 8
3.	K — B 1	P — Kt 4
4.	K — B 2	P — R 7
5.	Kt — K 3	P — Kt 5
6.	Kt — B 1	P — Kt 6 ch
7.	Kt × P mate	

Now that we have seen these exceptional cases, we can analyse the different merits and the relative value of the Knight and the Bishop.

It is generally thought by amateurs that the Knight is the more valuable piece of the two, the chief reason being that, unlike the Bishop, the Knight can command both Black and White squares. However, the fact is generally overlooked that the Knight, at any one time,

has the choice of one colour only.   It takes much longer
to bring a Knight from one wing to the other.   Also,
as shown in the following Example, a Bishop can
stalemate a Knight; a compliment which the Knight
is unable to return.

Example 32.

The weaker the player the more terrible the Knight
is to him, but as a player increases in strength the
value of the Bishop becomes more evident to him, and
of course there is, or should be, a corresponding decrease
in his estimation of the value of the Knight as compared
to the Bishop.   In this respect, as in many others, the
masters of to-day are far ahead of the masters of former
generations.   While not so long ago some of the very
best amongst them, like Pillsbury and Tchigorin, preferred Knights to Bishops, there is hardly a master of
to-day who would not completely agree with the state-
ments made above.

Example 33. — This is about the only case when the Knight is more valuable than the Bishop.

It is what is called a *"block position,"* and all the Pawns are on one side of the board. (If there were Pawns on both sides of the board there would be no advantage in having a Knight.) In such a position Black has excellent chances of winning. Of course, there is an extra source of weakness for White in having his Pawns on the same colour-squares as his Bishop. This is a mistake often made by players. The proper way, generally, in an ending, is to have your Pawns on squares of opposite colour to that of your own Bishop. When you have your Pawns on squares of the same colour the action of your own Bishop is limited by them, and consequently the value of the Bishop is diminished, since the value of a piece can often be measured by the number of squares it commands. While on this subject, I shall also call attention to the fact that it is generally preferable to keep your Pawns on squares of the same colour as that of the opposing Bishop, particularly if they are passed Pawns supported by the King.   The principles might be stated thus :

When the opponent has a Bishop, keep your Pawns on squares of the same colour as your opponent's Bishop.

Whenever you have a Bishop, whether the opponent has also one or not, keep your Pawns on squares of the opposite colour to that of your own Bishop.

Naturally, these principles have sometimes to be modified to suit the exigencies of the position.

Example 34. — In the following position the Pawns are on one side of the board, and there is no advantage in having either a Knight or a Bishop.   The game should surely end in a draw.

Example 35. — Now let us add three Pawns on each side to the above position, so that there are Pawns on both sides of the board.

It is now preferable to have the Bishop, though the position, if properly played out, should end in a draw. The advantage of having the Bishop lies as much in its ability to command, at long range, both sides of the board from a central position as in its ability to move quickly from one side of the board to the other.

Example 36 — In the above position it is unquestionably an advantage to have the Bishop, because, although each player has the same number of Pawns, they are not balanced on each side of the board. Thus, on the King's side, White has three to two, while on the Queen's side it is Black that has three to two. Still, with proper play, the game should end in a draw, though White has somewhat better chances.

Example 37. — Here is a position in which to have the Bishop is a decided advantage, since not

only are there Pawns on both sides of the board, but there is a passed Pawn (K R P for White, Q R P for Black). Black should have extreme difficulty in drawing this position, if he can do it at all.

Example 38. — Again Black would have great difficulty in drawing this position.

The student should carefully consider these positions. I hope that the many examples will help him
to understand, in their true value, the relative merits
of the Knight and Bishop. As to the general method
of procedure, a teacher, or practical experience, will
be best. I might say generally, however, that the
proper course in these endings, as in all similar endings, is: Advance of the King to the centre of the
board or towards the passed Pawns, or Pawns that
are susceptible of being attacked, and rapid advance
of the passed Pawn or Pawns as far as is consistent
with their safety.

To give a fixed line of play would be folly. Each
ending is different, and requires different handling,
according to what the adversary proposes to do.
Calculation by visualising the future positions is what
will count.

15. HOW TO MATE WITH A KNIGHT AND A BISHOP

Now, before going back again to the middle-game and the openings, let us see how to mate with Knight and Bishop, and, then, how to win with a Queen against a Rook.

With a Knight and a Bishop *the mate can only be given in the corners of the same colour as the Bishop.*

Example 39. — In this example we must mate either at Q R I or K R 8. The ending can be divided into two parts. Part one consists in driving the Black King to the last line. We might begin, as is generally done in all such cases, by advancing the King to the centre of the board :

I. K — K 2	K — Q 2

Black, in order to make it more difficult, goes towards the white-squared corner :

2. K — Q 3	K — B 3
3. B — B 4	K — Q 4

4.	Kt — K 2		K — B 4
5.	Kt — B 3		K — Kt 5
6.	K — Q 4		K — R 4
7.	K — B 5		K — R 3
8.	K — B 6		K — R 2
9.	Kt — Q 5		K — R 1

The first part is now over; the Black King is in the white-squared corner.

The second and last part will consist in driving the Black King now from Q R 8 to Q R 1 or K R 8 in order to mate him. Q R 1 will be the quickest in this position.

10.	Kt — Kt 6 ch		K — R 2
11.	B — B 7		K — R 3
12.	B — Kt 8		K — R̄ 4
13.	Kt — Q 5		K — R 5

Black tries to make for K R 1 with his King. White has two ways to prevent that, one by 14 B — K 5,

K — Kt 6; 15 Kt — K 3, and the other which I give as the text, and which I consider better for the student to learn, because it is more methodical and more in accord with the spirit of all these endings, *by using the King as much as possible.*

14.	K — B 5 !	K — Kt 6
15.	Kt — Kt 4	K — B 6
16.	B — B 4	K — Kt 6
17.	B — K 5	K — R 5
18.	K — B 4	K — R 4
19.	B — B 7 ch	K — R 5
20.	Kt — Q 3	K — R 6
21.	B — Kt 6	K — R 5
22.	Kt — Kt 2 ch	K — R 6
23.	K — B 3	K — R 7
24.	K — B 2	K — R 6
25.	B — B 5 ch	K — R 7
26.	Kt — Q 3	K — R 8
27.	B — Kt 4	K — R 7
28.	Kt — B 1 ch	K — R 8
29.	B — B 3 mate	

It will be seen that the ending is rather laborious. There are two outstanding features: the close following by the King, and the controlling of the squares of opposite colour to the Bishop by the combined action of the Knight and King. The student would do well to exercise himself methodically in this ending, as it gives a very good idea of the actual power of the pieces, and it requires foresight in order to accomplish the mate within the fifty moves which are granted by the rules.

16. QUEEN AGAINST ROOK

This is one of the most difficult endings without Pawns. The resources of the defence are many, and when used skilfully only a very good player will prevail within the limit of fifty moves allowed by the rules. (The rule is that at any moment you may demand that your opponent mate you within fifty moves. However, every time a piece is exchanged or a Pawn advanced the counting must begin afresh.)

Example 40. — This is one of the standard positions which Black can often bring about. Now, it is White's move. If it were Black's move it would be simple, as

he would have to move his Rook away from the King (find out why), and then the Rook would be comparatively easy to win. We deduce from the above that the main object is to force the Black Rook away from the defending King, and that, in order to compel Black to do so, we must bring about the position in the diagram with *Black* to move. Once we know what is required, the way to proceed becomes easier to find. Thus:

1. Q — K 5 ch

Not 1 Q — R 6, because R — B 2 ch; 2 K — Kt 6, R — B 3 ch; 3 K × R. Stalemate. (The beginner will invariably fall into this trap.)

1.	K to R 1 or to R 2
2. Q — R 1 ch	K — Kt 1
3. Q — R 5	

In a few moves we have accomplished our object. The first part is concluded. Now we come to the second part. The Rook can only go to a White square, otherwise the first check with the Queen will win it. Therefore

3.	R — Kt 6
4. Q — K 5 ch	K — R 1 best
5. Q — R 8 ch	K — R 2
6. Q — Kt 7 ch	K — R 1
7. Q — Kt 8 ch	R — Kt 1
8. Q — R 2 mate	

(The student should find out by himself how to win when 3...R — Kt 8; 4 Q — K 5 ch, K — R 2.)

Example 41. — The procedure here is very similar. The things to bear in mind are that the Rook must be prevented from interposing at Kt 1 because of an immediate mate, and in the same way the King must be prevented from going either to R 3 or B 1.

Example 42. — We shall now examine a more difficult position.

Many players would be deceived by this position. The most likely looking move is not the best. Thus suppose we begin

1. Q — K 5 ch   K — B 1
2. K — Kt 6   R — Q 2

The only defence, but, unfortunately, a very effective one, which makes it very difficult for White, since he cannot play 3 Q — K 6 because of 3...R — Kt 2 ch; 4 K — B 6, R — Kt 3 ch draws. Nor can he win quickly by 3 Q — Q B 5 ch because 3...K — K 1, 4 K — B 6, R — Q 3 ch! driving back the White King.

Now that we have seen the difficulties of the situation let us go back. The best move is

1. Q — Kt 5 ch!   K — R 1

If K — R 2; 2 Q — Kt 6 ch, K — R 1; 3 K — R 6!

2. Q — K 5 ch!   K — R 2 best
3. K — Kt 5   R — R 2 ! best

If 3...R — Kt 2 ch; 4 K — B 6 leads to a position similar to those in Examples 40 and 41.

4. Q — K 4 ch   K — Kt 1
5. Q — B 4 ch   K — R 2
6. K — B 6   R — K Kt 2
7. Q — R 4 ch   K — Kt 1
8. Q — R 5

and we have the position of Example 40 with Black to move.

Let us go back again.

    1. Q — Kt 5 ch   K — B 1
    2. Q — Q 8 ch   K — Kt 2
    3. K — Kt 5   R — B 6

The best place for the Rook away from the King. 3...K — R 2; 4 Q — Q 4, R — Kt 2 ch; 5 K — B 6 would lead to positions similar to those already seen.

    4. Q — Q 4 ch   K — B 1
    5. K — Kt 6

5 Q — Q 6 ch, K — Kt 2; 6 Q — K 5 ch, K — B 1; 7 K — Kt 6 would also win the Rook. The text move, however, is given to show the finesse of such endings. White now threatens mate at Q 8.

    5. ....   R — Kt 6 ch
    6. K — B 6   R — B 6 ch
    7. K — K 6   R — K R 6

White threatened mate at K R 8.

    8. Q — B 4 ch

and the Rook is lost.

Note, in these examples, that the checks at long range along the diagonals have often been the key to all the winning manœuvres. Also that the Queen and

King are often kept on different lines. The student should carefully go over these positions and consider all the possibilities not given in the text.

He should once more go through everything already written before proceeding further with the book.

CHAPTER III

Planning a Win in Middle-Game Play

I shall now give a few winning positions taken from my own games. I have selected those that I believe can be considered as *types*, i.e. positions that may easily occur again in a somewhat similar form. A knowledge of such positions is of great help; in fact, one cannot know too many. It often may help the player to find, with little effort, the right move, which he might not be able to find at all without such knowledge.

17. ATTACKING WITHOUT THE AID OF KNIGHTS

Example 43. — It is Black's move, and as he is a Kt and P behind he must win quickly, if at all. He plays:

1. .... Q R — Kt 1!
2. R — B 2

If, Q × Q, R × P ch; K — R 1, B — Q 4 and mate follows in a few moves.

2. .... R × P ch
3. K — B 1 B — B 5 ch
4. Kt × B R — Kt 8 mate

Example 44. — Black's last move was P — K 6, played with the object of stopping what he thought was White's threat, viz.. R — Q R 5, to which he would have answered Q — B 5 ch and drawn the game by perpetual check. White, however, has a more forceful move, and he mates in three moves as fo. lows:

1. R × P ch	Q × R
2. R — Q R 5	Black moves
3. White mates	

Example 45. — White has a beautiful position, but still he had better gain some material, if he can, before Black consolidates his defensive position. He therefore plays:

1. R × Kt !	P × R
2. B × P ch	K — K 2

If Kt × B; R × Kt and Black would be helpless.

3. Q — R 7 ch	K — K 1
4. Q × Kt ch	K — Q 2
5. Q — R 7 ch	Q — K 2
6. B — B 8	Q × Q
7. R × Q ch	K — K 1
8. R × R	Resigns

In these few examples the attacking has been done by Rooks and Bishops in combination with the Queen.

There have been no Knights to take part in the attack. We shall now give some examples in which the Knights play a prominent part as an attacking force.

18. ATTACKING WITH KNIGHTS AS A PROMINENT FORCE

Example 46. — White is two Pawns behind. He must therefore press on his attack. The game continues :

1. Kt (B 5) × Kt P   Kt — B 4

Evidently an error which made the winning easier for White, as he simply took the Rook with the Knight and kept up the attack. Black should have played : 1...Kt × Kt. Then would have followed : 2 Kt — B 6 ch, K — Kt 3 ; 3 Kt × B, P — B 3 (best) ; 4 P — K 5, K — B 2 ; 5 Kt × P, R — K 2 ; 6 Kt — K 4, and Black should lose.[1]

[1] Full score and notes are given in My Chess Career, by J. R. Capablanca (Game No. 11).

Example 47. — The student should carefully examine the position, as the sacrifice of the Bishop in similar situations is typical, and the chance for it is of frequent occurrence in actual play. The game continues:

1.	B × P ch	K × B
2.	Kt — Kt 5 ch	K — Kt 3

Best. If 2...K — R 3; 3 Kt × P ch wins the Queen, and if 2...K — Kt 1; 3 Q — R 5, with an irresistible attack.

3.	Q — Kt 4	P — B 4
4.	Q — Kt 3	K — R 3

White finally won.[1]

[1] This position is elaborated under Example 50 (p 80.).

19. WINNING BY INDIRECT ATTACK

We have so far given positions where the attacks were of a violent nature and directed against the King's position. Very often, however, in the middle-game attacks are made against a position or against pieces, or even Pawns.

The winning of a Pawn among good players of even strength often means the winning of the game.

Hence the study of such positions is of great importance. We give below two positions in which the attack aims at the gain of a mere Pawn as a means of ultimately winning the game.

Example 48. — Black is a Pawn behind, and there is no violent direct attack against White's King. Black's pieces, however, are very well placed and free to act, and by co-ordinating the action of all his pieces he is soon able not only to regain the Pawn but to obtain the better game. The student should carefully

consider this position and the subsequent moves. It is a very good example of proper co-ordination in the management of forces. The game continues:

    1. ....   R — R 1
    2. P — Q R 4

White's best move was P — Q Kt 3, when would follow Kt × B; 3 Q × Kt, R — R 6 and Black would ultimately win the Q R P, always keeping a slight advantage in position. The text move makes matters easier.

    2. ....   Kt × B
    3. Q × Kt   Q — B 5
    4. K R — Q 1   K R — Kt 1

Black could have regained the Pawn by playing B × Kt, but he sees that there is more to be had, and therefore increases the pressure against White's Queen side. He now threatens, among other things, R × Kt P.

    5. Q — K 3   R — Kt 5

Threatening to win the exchange by B — Q 5.

    6. Q — Kt 5   B — Q 5 ch
    7. K — R 1   Q R — Kt 1

This threatens to win the Kt, and thus forces White to give up the exchange.

    8. R × B   Q × R
    9. R — Q 1   Q — B 5

Now Black will recover his Pawn.

Example 49. — An examination of this position will show that Black's main weakness lies in the exposed position of his King, and in the fact that his Q R has not yet come into the game. Indeed, if it were Black's move, we might conclude that he would have the better game, on account of having three Pawns to two on the Queen's side, and his Bishop commanding the long diagonal.

It is, however, White's move, and he has two courses to choose from. The obvious move, B — B 4, might be good enough, since after 1 B — B 4, Q R — Q 1; 2 P — Q Kt 4 would make it difficult for Black. But there is another move which completely upsets Black's position and wins a Pawn, besides obtaining the better position. That move is Kt — Q 4! The game continues as follows:

1.	Kt — Q 4 !	P × Kt
2.	R × B	Kt — Kt 5

There is nothing better, as White threatened B — B 4.

3.	B — B 4 ch	K — R 1
4.	R — K 6	P — Q 6
5.	R × P	

And White, with the better position, is a Pawn ahead.

These positions have been given with the idea of acquainting the student with different types of combinations. I hope they will also help to develop his imagination, a very necessary quality in a good player. The student should note, in all these middle-game positions, that —

once the opportunity is offered, all the 'pieces are thrown into action " en masse" when necessary; and that *all the pieces smoothly co-ordinate their action with machine-like precision.*

That, at least, is what the ideal middle-game play should be, if it is not so altogether in these examples.

CHAPTER IV

GENERAL THEORY

BEFORE we revert to the technique of the openings it will be advisable to dwell a little on general theory, so that the openings in their relation to the rest of the game may be better understood.

20. THE INITIATIVE

As the pieces are set on the board both sides have the same position and the same amount of material. White, however, has the move, and the move in this case means *the initiative*, and the initiative, other things being equal, is an advantage. Now this advantage must be kept as long as possible, and should only be given up if some other advantage, material or positional, is obtained in its place. White, according to the principles already laid down, develops his pieces as fast as possible, but in so doing he also tries to hinder his opponent's development, by applying pressure wherever possible. He tries first of all to control the centre, and failing this to obtain some positional advantage that will make it possible for him to keep on harassing the enemy. He only relinquishes the initiative when he gets for it some material advantage under such favourable conditions as to make him feel assured that he will, in turn, be able to withstand his adversary's thrust; and finally, through his superiority of material, once more resume the initiative, which alone can give him the victory. This last assertion is self-evident, since, in order to win the game, the opposing King must be driven to a position where he is attacked without having any way of escape. Once the pieces have been properly developed the resulting positions may vary in character. It may be that a direct attack against the King is in order; or that it is a case of improving a position already advantageous; or, finally, that some material can be gained at the cost of relinquishing the initiative for a more or less prolonged period.

21. DIRECT ATTACKS *EN MASSE*

In the first case the attack must be carried on with sufficient force to guarantee its success. Under no consideration must a direct attack against the King be carried on *à outrance* unless there is absolute certainty in one's own mind that it will succeed, since failure in such cases means disaster.

Example 50. — A good example of a successful direct attack against the King is shown in the following diagram:

In this position White could simply play B — B 2 and still have the better position, but instead he prefers an immediate attack on the King's side, with the certainty in his mind that the attack will lead to a win. The game continues thus:[1]

12.	B × P ch	K × B
13.	Kt — Kt 5 ch	K — Kt 3
14.	Q — Kt 4	P — B 4

Best. P — K 4 would have been immediately fatal. Thus: 14...P — K 4; 15 Kt — K 6 ch, K — B 3; 16 P — B 4! P — K 5; 17 Q — Kt 5 ch, K × Kt; 18 Q — K 5 ch, K — Q 2; 19 K R — Q 1 ch, Kt — Q 6; 20 Kt × P, K — B 3 (if K — K 1, Kt — Q 6 ch wins the Queen); 21 R × Kt, Q × R; 22 R — B 1 ch, K — Kt 3 (if K — Q 2 mate in two); 23 Q — B 7 ch and mate in five moves.

[1] We give, from now on, games and notes, so that the student may familiarise himself with the many and varied considerations that constantly are borne in mind by the Chess Master. We must take it for granted that the student has already reached a stage where, while not being able fully to understand every move, yet he can derive benefit from any discussion with regard to them.

15.	Q — Kt 3	K — R 3
16.	Q — R 4 ch	K — Kt 3
17.	Q — R 7 ch	K — B 3

If K × Kt; Q × Kt P ch and mate in a few moves.

18.	P — K 4	Kt — Kt 3
19.	P × P	P × P
20.	Q R — Q 1	Kt — Q 6
21.	Q — R 3	Kt (Q 6) — B 5
22.	Q — Kt 3	Q — B 2
23.	K R — K 1	Kt — K 7 ch

This blunder loses at once, but the game could not be saved in any case; e.g. 23...B — K 3; 24 R × B ch, Kt × R; 25 Kt — Q 5 mate.

24.	R × Kt	Q × Q
25.	Kt — R 7 ch	K — B 2
26.	R P × Q	R — R 1
27.	Kt — Kt 5 ch	K — B 3
28.	P — B 4	Resigns

Example 51. — Another example of this kind:

In the above position the simple move Kt × P would win, but White looks for complications and their beauties. Such a course is highly risky until a wide experience of actual master-play has developed a sufficient insight into all the possibilities of a position. This game, which won the brilliancy prize at St. Petersburg in 1914, continued as follows: —

21.	B — R 4	Q — Q 2
22.	Kt × B	Q × R
23.	Q — Q 8 ch	Q — K 1

If K — B 2; 24 Kt — Q 6 ch, King moves; 25 mate.

24.	B — K 7 ch	K — B 2
25.	Kt — Q 6 ch	K — Kt 3
26.	Kt — R 4 ch	K — R 4

If 26...K — R 3; 27 Kt (Q 6) — B 5 ch, K — R 4; 28 Kt × P ch, K — R 3; 29 Kt (R 4) — B 5 ch, K — Kt 3; 30 Q — Q 6 ch and mate next move.

27.	Kt × Q	R × Q
28.	Kt × P ch	K — R 3
29.	Kt (Kt 7) — B 5 ch	K — R 4
30.	P — K R 3 !	

The climax of the combination started with 21 B — R 4. White is still threatening mate, and the best way to avoid it is for Black to give back all the material he has gained and to remain three Pawns behind.

The student should note that in the examples given the attack is carried out with every available piece, and that often, as in some of the variations pointed out, it is the coming into action of the last available piece that finally overthrows the enemy. It demonstrates the principle already stated:

Direct and violent attacks against the King must be carried en masse, with full force, to ensure their success. The opposition must be overcome at all cost; the attack cannot be broken off, since in all such cases that means defeat.

22. THE FORCE OF THE THREATENED ATTACK

Failing an opportunity, in the second case, for direct attack, one must attempt to increase whatever weakness there may be in the opponent's position; or, if there is none, one or more must be created. It is always an advantage to threaten something, but such threats must be carried into effect only if something is to be gained immediately. For, holding the threat in hand, forces the opponent to provide against its execution and to keep material in readiness to meet it. Thus he may more easily overlook, or be unable to parry, a thrust at another point. But once the threat is carried into effect, it exists no longer, and your opponent can devote his attention to his own schemes. One of the best and most successful manœuvres in this type of game is to make a demonstration on one side, so as to draw the forces of your opponent to that side, then through the greater mobility of your pieces to shift your forces quickly

to the other side and break through, before your
opponent has had the time to bring over the necessary forces for the defence.

A good example of positional play is shown in the
following game :

Example 52.— Played at the Havana International Masters Tournament, 1913. (French Defence.)
White : J. R. Capablanca. Black : R. Blanco.

1.	P — K 4	P — K 3
2.	P — Q 4	P — Q 4
3.	Kt — Q B 3	P × P
4.	Kt × P	Kt — Q 2
5.	Kt — K B 3	K Kt — B 3
6.	Kt × Kt ch	Kt × Kt
7.	Kt — K 5	

This move was first shown to me by the talented
Venezuelan amateur, M. Ayala. The object is to

prevent the development of Black's Queen's Bishop *viâ* Q Kt 2, after P — Q Kt 3, which is Black's usual development in this variation. Generally it is bad to move the same piece twice in an opening before the other pieces are out, and the violation of that principle is the only objection that can be made to this move, which otherwise has everything to recommend it.

7. .... B — Q 3
8. Q — B 3

B — K Kt 5 might be better. The text move gives Black an opportunity of which he does not avail himself

8. .... P — B 3

P — B 4 was the right move. It would have led to complications, in which Black might have held his own; at least, White's play would be very difficult. The text move accomplishes nothing, and puts Black in an altogether defensive position. The veiled threat B × Kt; followed by Q — R 4 ch; is easily met.

9.	P — B 3	O — O
10.	B — K Kt 5	B — K 2

The fact that Black has now to move his Bishop back clearly demonstrates that Black's plan of development is faulty. He has lost too much time, and White brings his pieces into their most attacking position without hindrance of any sort.

11.	B — Q 3	Kt — K 1

The alternative was Kt — Q 4. Otherwise White would play Q — R 3, and Black would be forced to play P — K Kt 3 (not P — K R 3, because of the sacrifice B × P), seriously weakening his King's side.

12.	Q — R 3	P — K B 4

White has no longer an attack, but he has compelled Black to create a marked weakness. Now White's whole plan will be to exploit this weakness (the weak K P), and the student can now see how the principles expounded previously are applied in this game. Every move is directed to make the weak King's Pawn untenable, or to profit by the inactivity of the Black pieces defending the Pawn, in order to improve the position of White at other points.

13.	B × B	Q × B
14.	O — O	R — B 3
15.	K R — K 1	Kt — Q 3
16.	R — K 2	B — Q 2

At last the Bishop comes out, not as an active attacking piece, but merely to make way for the Rook.

    17.   Q R — K 1   R — K 1
    18.   P — Q B 4   Kt — B 2

A very clever move, tending to prevent P — B 5, and tempting White to play Kt × B, followed by B × P, which would be bad, as the following variation shows: 19 Kt × B, Q × Kt; 20 B × P, Kt— Kt 4; 21 Q — Kt 4, R × B; 22 P — K R 4, P— K R 4; 23 Q × R, P × Q; 24 R × R ch, K — R 2; 25 P × Kt, Q × P. But it always happens in such cases that, if one line of attack is anticipated, there is another; and this is no exception to the rule, as will be seen.

    19.   P — Q 5 !   Kt × Kt

Apparently the best way to meet the manifold threats of White. B P × P would make matters worse, as the White Bishop would finally bear on the weak King's Pawn *via* Q B 4.

20.	R × Kt	P — K Kt 3
21.	Q — R 4	K — Kt 2
22.	Q — Q 4	P — B 4

Forced, as White threatened P × K P, and also Q × P

| 23. | Q — B 3 | P — Kt 3 |

Q — Q 3 was better. But Black wants to tempt
White to play P × P, thinking that he will soon after
regain his Pawn with a safe position. Such, however,
is not the case, as White quickly demonstrates. I
must add that in any case Black's position is, in my
opinion, untenable, since all his pieces are tied up for
the defence of a Pawn, while White's pieces are free
to act.

| 24. | P × P | B — B 1 |

25. B — K 2 !

The deciding and timely manœuvre. All the Black
pieces are useless after this Bishop reaches Q 5.

25.	....	B × P
26.	B — B 3	K — B 2
27.	B — Q 5	Q — Q 3

Now it is evident that all the Black pieces are tied up, and it only remains for White to find the quickest way to force the issue. White will now try to place his Queen at K R 6, and then advance the K R P to R 5 in order to break up the Black Pawns defending the King.

28.	Q — K 3	R — K 2

If 28...P — B 5; 29 Q — K R 3, P — K R 4; 30 Q — R 4, R — K 2; 31 Q — Kt 5, K — Kt 2; 32 P — K R 4, Q — Q 2; 33 P — K Kt 3, P × P; 34 P — B 4, and Black will soon be helpless, as he has to mark time with his pieces while White prepares to advance P — R 5, and finally at the proper time to play R × B, winning.

29.	Q — R 6	K — Kt 1
30.	P — K R 4	P — R 3
31.	P — R 5	P — B 5
32.	P × P	P × P
33.	R × B	Resigns.

Commenting on White's play in this game, Dr. E. Lasker said at the time that if White's play were properly analysed it might be found that there was no way to improve upon it.

These apparently simple games are often of the most difficult nature. Perfection in such cases is much more difficult to obtain than in those positions calling for a brilliant direct attack against the King, involving sacrifices of pieces.

23. RELINQUISHING THE INITIATIVE

In the third case, there is nothing to do, once the material advantage is obtained, but to submit to the opponent's attack for a while, and once it has been repulsed to act quickly with all your forces and win on material. A good example of this type of game is given below.

Example 53. — From the Havana International Masters Tournament, 1913. (Ruy Lopez.) White: J. R. Capablanca. Black: D. Janowski.

1.	P — K 4	P — K 4
2.	Kt — K B 3	Kt — Q B 3
3.	B — Kt 5	Kt — B 3
4.	O — O	P — Q 3
5.	B × Kt ch	P × B
6.	P — Q 4	B — K 2
7.	Kt — B 3	

P × P might be better, but at the time I was not familiar with that variation, and therefore I played what I knew to be good.

7.	....	Kt — Q 2
8.	P × P	P × P
9.	Q — K 2	O — O
10.	R — Q 1	B — Q 3
11.	B — Kt 5	Q — K 1
12.	Kt — K R 4	P — Kt 3

Black offers the exchange in order to gain time and to obtain an attack. Without considering at all whether or not such a course was justified on the part of Black, it is evident that as far as White is concerned there is only one thing to do, viz., to win the exchange and then prepare to weather the storm. Then, once it is passed, to act quickly with all forces to derive the benefit of numerical superiority.

13.	B — R 6	Kt — B 4
14.	R — Q 2	R — Kt 1
15.	Kt — Q 1	R — Kt 5

To force White to play P — Q B 4, and thus create a hole at Q 5 for his Knight.[1] Such grand tactics show the hand of a master.

16.	P — Q B 4	Kt — K 3
17.	B × R	Q × B
18.	Kt — K 3	

Kt — K B 3 was better.

18.	....	Kt — Q 5
19.	Q — Q 1	P — Q B 4

In order to prevent R × Kt giving back the exchange, but winning a Pawn and relieving the position.

20.	P — Q Kt 3	R — Kt 1

In order to play B — Kt 2 without blocking his Rook.

[1] A "hole" in chess parlance has come to mean a defect in Pawn formation which allows the opponent to establish his forces in wedge formation or otherwise without the possibility of dislodging him by Pawn moves. Thus, in the following diagram, Black has two "holes" at K B 3 and K R 3, where White forces, e.g. a Kt or B, could establish themselves, supported by pieces or Pawns.

Black's manœuvring for positional advantage is ad-
mirable throughout this game, and if he loses it is
due entirely to the fact that the sacrifice of the exchange,
without even a Pawn for it, could not succeed against
sound defensive play.

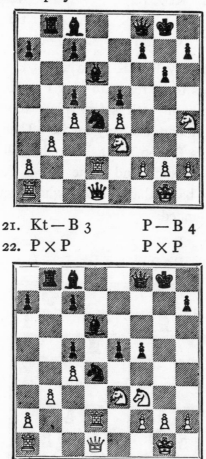

21. Kt — B 3   P — B 4
22. P × P   P × P

The position begins to look really dangerous for White.
In reality Black's attack is reaching its maximum
force. Very soon it will reach the apex, and then

White, who is well prepared, will begin his counter action, and through his superiority in material obtain an undoubted advantage.

23.	Kt — B 1	P — B 5
24.	Kt × Kt	B P × Kt
25.	Q — R 5	B — Kt 2
26.	R — K 1	P — B 4

He could not play R — K 1 because of R × Q P. Besides, he wants to be ready to play P — K 5. At present White cannot with safety play R × K P, but he will soon prepare the way for it. Then, by giving up a Rook for a Bishop and a Pawn, he will completely upset Black's attack and come out a Pawn ahead. It is on this basis that White's whole defensive manoeuvre is founded.

27.	P — B 3	R — K 1
28.	R (Q 2) — K 2	R — K 3

Now the Black Rook enters into the game, but White is prepared. It is now time to give back the exchange.

29. R × P	B × R
30. R × B	R — K R 3
31. Q — K 8	Q × Q
32. R × Q ch	K — B 2
33. R — K 5	R — Q B 3
34. Kt — Q 2	

R — B 5 ch might have been better. The text move did not prove as strong as anticipated.

34.	K — B 3
35. R — Q 5	R — K 3
36. Kt — K 4 ch	K — K 2

R × Kt would lose easily

37. R × B P	P — Q 6 !

Very fine. White cannot play R   B 7 ch because of K — Q 1; R × B, R × Kt winning.

38. K — B 2	B × Kt
39. P × B	R × P
40. R — Q 5	R — K 6

The ending is very difficult to win. At this point White had to make the last move before the game was adjourned.

41.	P — Q Kt 4 !	R — K 5
42.	R × P	R × P
43.	R — K R 3	R × P
44.	R × P ch	K — B 3
45.	R × P	K — B 4
46.	K — B 3	R — Kt 7
47.	R — R 5 ch	K — B 3
48.	R — R 4	K — Kt 4
49.	R × P	R × R P
50.	P — R 4 ch	K — R 4
51.	R — B 5 ch	K — R 3
52.	P — Kt 4	Resigns

I have passed over the game lightly because of its difficult nature, and because we are at present concerned more with the opening and the middle-game than we are with the endings, which will be treated separately.

24. CUTTING OFF PIECES FROM THE SCENE OF ACTION

Very often in a game a master only plays to cut off, so to speak, one of the pieces from the scene of actual conflict. Often a Bishop or a Knight is completely put out of action. In such cases we might say that from that moment the game is won, because for all practical purposes there will be one more piece on one side than on the other. A very good illustration is furnished by the following game.

Example 54. — Played at the Hastings Victory Tournament, 1919. (Four Knights.) White: **W. Winter.** Black: J. R. Capablanca.

1.	P — K 4	P — K 4
2.	Kt — K B 3	Kt — Q B 3
3.	Kt — B 3	Kt — B 3
4.	B — Kt 5	B — Kt 5
5.	O — O	O — O
6.	B × Kt	

Niemzowitch's variation, which I have played successfully in many a game. It gives White a very solid game. Niemzowitch's idea is that White will in due time be able to play P — K B 4, opening a line for his Rooks, which, in combination with the posting of a Knight at K B 5, should be sufficient to win. He thinks that should Black attempt to stop the Knight from going to K B 5, he will have to weaken his game in some other way. Whether this is true or not remains to be proved, but in my opinion the move is perfectly good. On the other hand, there is no question that Black can easily develop his pieces. But it must be considered that in this variation White does not attempt to hinder Black's development, he simply attempts to build up a position which he considers impregnable and from which he can start an attack in due course.

6.	....	Q P × B

The alternative, Kt P × B; gives White the best of the game, without doubt.[1]

| 7. P — Q 3 | B — Q 3 |
| 8. B — Kt 5 | |

This move is not at all in accordance with the nature of this variation. The general strategical plan for White is to play P — K R 3, to be followed in time by the advance of the K Kt P to Kt 4, and the bringing of the Q Kt to K B 5 via K 2 and K Kt 3 or Q 1 and K 3. Then, if possible, the K Kt is linked with the other Kt by placing it at either K R 4, K Kt 3, or K 3 as the occasion demands. The White King sometimes remains at Kt 1, and other times it is placed at K Kt 2, but mostly at K R 1. Finally, in most cases comes P — K B 4, and then the real attack begins. Sometimes it is a direct assault against the King,[2] and at other times it comes simply to finessing for positional advantage in the end-game, after most of the pieces have been exchanged.[3]

| 8. .... | P — K R 3 |
| 9. B — R 4 | P — B 4 |

[1] See game Capablanca-Kupchick, from Havana International Masters Tournament Book, 1913, by J. R. Capablanca; or a game in the Carlsbad Tournament of 1911, Vidmar playing Black against Alechin.

[2] See Niemzowitch's game in the All Russian Masters Tournament, 1914, at St. Petersburg, against Levitzki, I believe.

[3] See Capablanca-Janowski game, New York Masters Tournament, 1913.

To prevent P — Q 4 and to draw White into playing
Kt — Q 5, which would prove fatal. Black's plan is
to play P — K Kt 4, as soon as the circumstances
permit, in order to free his Queen and Knight from
the pin by the Bishop.

10. Kt — Q 5

White falls into the trap. Only lack of experience
can account for this move. White should have considered that a player of my experience and strength
could never allow such a move if it were good.

10. . . . .   P — K Kt 4

After this move White's game is lost. White cannot play Kt × Kt P, because Kt × Kt will win a piece. Therefore he must play B — Kt 3, either before or after Kt × Kt, with disastrous results in either case, as will be seen.

11.	Kt × Kt ch	Q × Kt
12.	B — Kt 3	B — Kt 5
13.	P — K R 3	B × Kt
14.	Q × B	Q × Q
15.	P × Q	P — K B 3

A simple examination will show that White is minus a Bishop for all practical purposes. He can only free it by sacrificing one Pawn, and possibly not even then. At least it would lose time besides the Pawn. Black now devotes all his energy to the Queen's side, and, having practically a Bishop more, the result cannot be in doubt. The rest of the game is given, so that the student may see how simple it is to win such a game.

16.	K — Kt 2	P — Q R 4
17.	P — Q R 4	K — B 2
18.	R — R 1	K — K 3
19.	P — R 4	K R — Q Kt 1

There is no necessity to pay any attention to the King's side, because White gains nothing by exchanging Pawns and opening the King's Rook file.

20.	P × P	R P × P
21.	P — Kt 3	P — B 3
22.	R — Q R 2	P — Kt 4
23.	K R — R 1	P — B 5

If White takes the proffered Pawn, Black regains it immediately by R — Kt 5, after P × B P.

24.	R P × P	P × P (Kt 6)
25.	B P × P	R × P
26.	R — R 4	R × P
27.	P — Q 4	R — Kt 4
28.	R — B 4	R — Kt 5
29.	R × B P	R × P
	Resigns	

25. A PLAYER'S MOTIVES CRITICISED IN A SPECIMEN GAME

Now that a few of my games with my own notes have been given, I offer for close perusal and study a very fine game played by Sir George Thomas, one of England's foremost players, against Mr. F. F. L. Alexander, in the championship of the City of London Chess Club in the winter of 1919–1920. It has the interesting feature for the student that Sir George Thomas kindly wrote the notes to the game for me at my request, and with the understanding that I would make the comments on them that I considered appropriate. Sir George Thomas' notes are in brackets and thus will be distinguished from my own comments.

Example 55. — Queen's Gambit Declined. (*The notes within brackets by Sir George Thomas.*) White: **Mr. F. F. L. Alexander.** Black: Sir George Thomas.

	White	Black
1.	P — Q 4	P — Q 4
2.	Kt — K B 3	Kt — K B 3
3.	P — B 4	P — K 3
4.	Kt — B 3	Q Kt — Q 2
5.	B — Kt 5	P — B 3
6.	P — K 3	Q — R 4

(One of the objects of Black's method of defence is to attack White's Q Kt doubly by Kt — K 5, followed by P × P. But 7 Kt — Q 2 is probably a strong way

of meeting this threat.) There are, besides, two good
reasons for this method of defence; first, that it is
not as much played as some of the other defences
and consequently not so well known, and second that
it leaves Black with two Bishops against B and Kt,
which, in a general way, constitutes an advantage.

7.	B × Kt	Kt × B
8.	P — Q R 3	Kt — K 5
9.	Q — Kt 3	B — K 2

This is not the logical place for the B which should
have been posted at Q 3. In the opening, time is of
great importance, and therefore the player should be
extremely careful in his development and make sure
that he posts his pieces in the right places.

10.	B — Q 3	Kt × Kt
11.	P × Kt	P × P
12.	B × B P	B — B 3

(I did not want White's Kt to come to K 5, from
where I could not dislodge it by P — K B 3 without
weakening my K P.) The same result could be accomplished by playing B — Q 3. Incidentally it bears
out my previous statement that the B should have
been originally played to Q 3.

13. O — O

The alternative was P — K 4, followed by P — K 5,
and then O — O. White would thereby assume the
initiative but would weaken his Pawn position considerably, and might be compelled to stake all on a

violent attack against the King. This is a turning point in the game, and it is in such positions that the temperament and style of the player decide the course of the game.

13. .... O—O
14. P—K 4 P—K 4

15. P—Q 5

(White might play 15 K R—Q 1, keeping the option of breaking up the centre later on. I wanted him to advance this P as there is now a fine post for my B at Q B 4.) By this move White shows that he does not understand the true value of his position. His only advantage consisted in the undeveloped condition of Black's Q B. He should therefore have made a plan to prevent the B from coming out, or if that were not possible, then he should try to force Black to weaken his Pawn position in order to come out with the B. There were three moves to consider: first,

P — Q R 4, in order to maintain the White B in the dominating position that it now occupies. This would have been met by Q — B 2; second, either of the Rooks to Q 1 in order to threaten 16 P × P, B × P; 17 Kt × B, Q × Kt; 18 B × P ch. This would have been met by B — Kt 5; and third, P — K R 3 to prevent B — Kt 5 and by playing either R to Q 1, followed up as previously stated to force Black to play P — Q Kt 4, which would weaken his Queen's side Pawns. Thus by playing P — K R 3 White would have attained the desired object. The text move blocks the action of the White B and facilitates Black's development. Hereafter White will act on the defensive, and the interest throughout the rest of the game will centre mainly on Black's play and the manner in which he carries out the attack.

15. ....   Q — B 2
16. B — Q 3

(This seems wrong, as it makes the development of Black's Queen wing easier. At present he cannot play P — Q Kt 3, because of the reply P × P followed by B — Q 5.)

16. ....   P — Q Kt 3
17. P — B 4   B — Kt 2
18. K R — B 1

(With the idea of Q R — Kt 1 and P — B 5. But it only compels Black to bring his B to Q B 4, which he would do in any case.)

18.	....	B — K 2
19.	R — B 2	B — B 4
20.	Q — Kt 2	P — B 3

(It would have been better, probably, to play 20...K R — K 1, with the idea of P — B 4 presently.) Black's play hereabout is weak; it lacks force, and there seems to be no well-defined plan of attack. It is true that these are the most difficult positions to handle in a game. In such cases a player must conceive a plan on a large scale, which promises chances of success, and with it all, it must be a plan that can be carried out with the means at his disposal. From the look of the position it seems that Black's best chance would be to mass his forces for an attack against White's centre, to be followed by a direct attack against the King. He should, therefore, play Q R — K 1, threatening P — K B 4. If White is able to defeat this plan, or rather to prevent it, then, once he has fixed some of the White pieces on the King's side, he should quickly shift his attack to the Queen's side, and open a line for his Rooks, which, once they enter in action, should produce an advantage on account of the great power of the two Bishops.

21.	Q R — Kt 1	Q R — Q 1
22.	P — Q R 4	B — R 3
23.	R — Q 1	

(White has clearly lost time with his Rook's moves.)

23.	....	K R — K 1
24.	Q — Kt 3	

(To bring his Queen across after Kt — R 4 and B — K 2.)

24. ....   R — Q 3
25. Kt — R 4   P — Kt 3
26. B — K 2

26. ....   P × P

(I thought this exchange necessary here, as White is threatening to play his Bishop via Kt 4 to K 6. If he retook with the Bishop's Pawn I intended to exchange Bishops and rely on the two Pawns to one on the Queen's wing. I did not expect him to retake it with the King's Pawn, which seemed to expose him to a violent King's side attack.) Black's judgment in this instance I believe to be faulty. Had White retaken with the B P, as he expected, he would have had the worst of the Pawn position, as White would have had a passed Pawn well supported on the Queen's side. His only advantage would lie in his having a very well posted Bishop against a badly posted Knight, and on the fact that in such positions as the above, the Bishop is invariably stronger than the Knight. He could and should have prevented all that, by playing B — B 1, as, had White then replied with Q — Kt 3, he could then play P × P, and White would not have been able to retake with the B P on account of B × P ch winning the exchange.

27.	K P × P	P — K 5
28.	P — Kt 3	P — K 6

I do not like this move. It would have been better to hold it in reserve and to have played P — B 4, to be followed in due time by P — K Kt 4 and P — B 5, after having placed the Q at Q 2, K B 2, or some other square as the occasion demanded. The text move blocks the action of the powerful B at Q B 4, and tends to make White's position safer than it should have been. The move in itself is a very strong attacking move, but it is isolated, and there is no effective continuation. Such advances as a rule should only be made when they can be followed by a concerted action of the pieces.

29.	P — B 4	B — B 1
30.	Kt — B 3	B — B 4
31.	R — Kt 2	R — K 5
32.	K — Kt 2	Q — B 1
33.	Kt — Kt 1	P — K Kt 4

(If now 34 B—B 3, P×P; 35 B×R, B×B ch, with a winning attack.)

34. P×P   P×P
35. R—K B 1   P—Kt 5

R—R 3 was the alternative. White's only move would have been K—R 1. The position now is evidently won for Black, and it is only a question of finding the right course. The final attack is now carried on by Sir George Thomas in an irreproachable manner.

36. B—Q 3   R—K B 3
37. Kt—K 2   Q—B 1

(Again preventing B × R, by the masked attack on White's Rook. White therefore protects his Rook.) If Kt—B 4, P—K 7!; 39 Kt×P, R×Kt ch; 40 R×R, B—K 5 ch!!; 41 B×B, best, R×R and White is lost. If, however, against 38 Kt—B 4, Black plays Q—R 3, and White 39 Q—B 2, I take pleasure in offering the position to my readers as a most beautiful and extraordinary win for Black, beginning with 39...Q—R 6 ch!!! I leave the variations for the student to work out.

  38. R (Kt 2) — Kt 1   Q—R 3
  39. Q—B 2

(Making a double attack on the Rook — which still cannot be taken — and preparing to defend the K R P.) If either the Rook or Bishop are taken White would be mated in a few moves.

  39. ....   Q—R 6 ch
  40. K—R 1   R × P!!

(If 40...R — R 3; 41 Kt — Kt 1, Q × Kt P; 42 Q — K Kt 2. Black therefore tries to get the Queen away from the defence.) A very beautiful move, and the best way to carry on the attack.

  41. Q × R

(The best defence was 41 R × B, but Black would emerge with Queen against Rook and Knight.)

          41. ....   B × B

(Again, not R — K R 3; because of P — Q 6 dis. ch.)

          42. R × R

(If 42 Q × B, then, at last, R — R 3 wins.)

          42. ....   B × Q
          43. Kt — B 4   P— K 7 !

(The Queen has no escape, but White has no time to take it.)

          44. R — K Kt 1   Q — B 8

White resigns. A very fine finish.

CHAPTER V

END-GAME STRATEGY

WE must now revert once more to the endings. Their importance will have become evident to the student who has taken the trouble to study my game with Janowski (Example 53). After an uneventful opening — a Ruy Lopez — in one of its normal variations, my opponent suddenly made things interesting by offering the exchange; an offer which, of course, I accepted. Then followed a very hard, arduous struggle, in which I had to defend myself against a very dangerous attack made possible by the excellent manœuvring of my adversary. Finally, there came the time when I could give back the material and change off most of the pieces, and come to an ending in which I clearly had the advantage. But yet the ending itself was not as simple as it at first appeared, and finally — perhaps through one weak move on my part — it became a very difficult matter to find a win. Had I been a weak end-game player the game would probably have ended in a draw, and all my previous efforts would have been in vain. Unfortunately, that is very often the case among the large majority of players; they are weak in the endings; a failing from which masters of the first rank are at times not free.

Incidentally, I might call attention to the fact that all the world's champions of the last sixty years have been exceedingly strong in the endings: Morphy, Steinitz, and Dr. Lasker had no superiors in this department of the game while they held their titles.

26. THE SUDDEN ATTACK FROM A DIFFERENT SIDE

I have previously stated, when speaking about general theory, that at times the way to win consists in attacking first on one side, then, granted greater mobility of the pieces, to transfer the attack quickly from one side to the other, breaking through before your opponent has been able to bring up sufficient forces to withstand the attack. This principle of the middle-game can sometimes be applied in the endings in somewhat similar manner.

Example 56.

In the above position I, with the **Black pieces,**
played:

1.	R — K 5 ch
2. R — K 2	R — Q R 5
3. R — R 2	P — K R 4

The idea, as will be seen very soon, is to play P — R 5
in order to fix White's King's side Pawns with a view
to the future. It is evident to Black that White
wants to bring his King to Q Kt 3 to support his
two weak isolated Pawns, and thus to free his Rooks.
Black, therefore, makes a plan to shift the attack to
the King's side at the proper time, in order to obtain
some advantage from the greater mobility of his
Rooks.

4. R — Q 1	R (Q 4) — Q R 4

in order to force the Rook to Rook's square, keeping
both Rooks tied up.

5. R (Q 1) — R 1	P — R 5
6. K — Q 2	K — Kt 2
7. K — B 2	R — K Kt 4

Black begins to transfer his attack to the King's side.

8. R — K Kt 1

A serious mistake, which loses quickly. White should
have played 8 K — Kt 3, when Black would have
answered 8...R (R 5) — R 4; 9 P — B 3, and Black
would have obtained an opening at K Kt 6 for his
King, which in the end might give him the victory.

8.	R — K B 5

Now the King cannot go to Kt 3, because of R —
Kt 4 ch.

     9. K — Q 3   R — B 6 ch

    10. K — K 2

If P × R, R × R; followed by R — K R 8 winning,

    10. . . . .   R × R P

and Black won after a few moves.

Example 57. — Another good example, in which
is shown the advantage of the greater mobility of
the pieces in an ending, is the following from a game
Capablanca-Kupchick played at the Havana Masters
Tournament, 1913. The full score and notes of the
game can be found in the book of the tournament.

White's only advantage in the above position is that
he possesses the open file and has the move, which
will secure him the initiative. There is also the slight
advantage of having his Pawns on the Queen's side
united, while Black has an isolated Q R P. **The**

proper course, as in the previous ending, is to bring
the Rooks forward, so that at least one of them may
be able to shift from one side of the board to the
other, and thus keep Black's Rooks from moving
freely. What this means in general theory has been
stated already; it really means: *keep harassing the
enemy; force him to use his big pieces to defend Pawns.
If he has a weak point, try to make it weaker, or create
another weakness somewhere else and his position will
collapse sooner or later. If he has a weakness, and he
can get rid of it, make sure that you create another weakness somewhere else.*

From the position in question the game continued
thus:

1. R — K 4   K R — K 1

with the object of repeating White's manœuvre, and
also not to allow White the control of the open file.

2. Q R — K 1   R — K 3
3. Q R — K 3   R (B1) — K 1
4. K — B 1   K — B 1

Black wants to bring his King to the centre of the
board in order to be nearer to whatever point White
decides to attack. The move is justified at least on
the general rule that in such endings the King should
be in the middle of the board. He does nothing after
all but follow White's footsteps. Besides, it is hard
to point out anything better. If 4...P — Q 4; 5 R —
Kt 4 ch, followed by K — K 2, would leave Black in
a very disagreeable position. If 4...P — K B 4; 5 R —

Q 4 ! R × R? 6 P × R, R × P ; 7 K — B 2, R — K 2 ;
8 R — Q R 4, winning the Q R P, which would practically leave White with a passed Pawn ahead on the
Queen's side, as the three Pawns of Black on the
King's side would be held by the two of White.

5.	K — K 2	K — K 2
6.	R — Q R 4	R — Q R 1

The student should note that through the same manœuvre Black is forced into a position similar to the
one shown in the previous ending.

7. R — R 5 !

This move has a manifold object. It practically fixes
all of Black's Pawns except the Q P, which is the only
one that can advance two squares. It specially prevents the advance of Black's K B Pawns, and at the
same time threatens the advance of White's K B
Pawns to B 4 and B 5. By this threat it practically
forces Black to play P — Q 4, which is all White desires,
for reasons that will soon become evident.

7.	....	P — Q 4
8.	P – Q B 4 !	K — Q 3

Evidently forced, as the only other move to save a
Pawn would have been P × P, which would have left
all Black's Pawns isolated and weak. If 8...P — Q 5 ;
9 R — K 4, K — Q 3 ; 10 P — Q Kt 4 ! R — K 4 ;
11 R — R 6, and Black's game is hopeless.

9.	P — B 5 ch	K — Q 2
10.	P — Q 4	P — B 4

Apparently very strong, since it forces the exchange of Rooks because of the threat R — R 3; but in reality it leads to nothing. The best chance was to play R — K K 1.

    11. R × R   P × R
    12. P — B 4

Up to now White had played with finesse, but this last move is weak. R — R 6 was the proper way to continue, so as to force Black to give up his Q R P or Q B P.

    12. ....   K — B 1
    13. K — Q 2

Again a bad move. 13 R — R 3 was the proper continuation, and if then 13...R — Kt 1; 14 P — Kt 3, K — Kt 2; 15 P — Kt 4, K — R 1; 16 R — Q Kt 3, with excellent winning chances; in fact, I believe, a won game.

    13. ....   K — Kt 2

Black misses his only chance. R — Kt 1 would have drawn.

14.	R — R 3	R — K Kt 1
15.	R — R 3	R — Kt 2
16.	K — K 2	K — R 3
17.	R — R 6	R — K 2
18.	K — Q 3	K — Kt 2

He goes back with the King to support his K P, and thus be able to utilise his Rook. It is, however, useless, and only White's weak play later on gives him further chances of a draw.

| 19. | P — K R 4 | K — B 1 |
| 20. | R — R 5 | |

To prevent the Black Rook from controlling the open file

20.	....	K — Q 2
21.	R — Kt 5	R — B 2
22.	K — B 3	K — B 1

He must keep his King on that side because White threatens to march with his King to R 6 via Kt 4.

23.	K — Kt 4	R — B 3
24.	K — R 5	K — Kt 2
25.	P — R 4	P — Q R 3
26.	P — R 5	R — R 3

He can do nothing but wait for White. The text move stops White from moving his Rook, but only for one move.

| 27. | P — Kt 4 | R — B 3 |

The only other move was K — R 2; when White could play R — Kt 7, or even P — Kt 5.

28. P — Kt 5

A weak move, which gives Black a fighting chance. In this ending, as is often the case with most players, White plays the best moves whenever the situation is difficult and requires careful handling, but once his position seems to be overwhelming he relaxes his efforts and the result is nothing to be proud of. The right move was 28 R — Kt 7.

28.	....	R P × P
29.	P × P	R — B 1 !
30.	R — Kt 7	R — R 1 ch
31.	K — Kt 4	P × P
32.	K × P	R — R 7
33.	P — B 6 ch	K — Kt 1
34.	R × R P	R — Kt 7 ch
35.	K — R 5	R — R 7 ch
36.	K — Kt 4	R × P

Black misses his last chance: R — Kt 7 ch, forcing the King to B 3, in order to avoid the perpetual, would probably draw. The reader must bear in mind that my opponent was then a very young and inexperienced player, and consequently deserves a great deal of credit for the fight he put up.

37. R — K 7   R × P

R — Kt 7 ch; followed by R — K R 7, offered better chances.

38.	P — R 6 !	R × P ch
39.	K — Kt 5	R — Q 8
40.	P — R 7	R — Kt 8 ch
41.	K — B 5	R — B 8 ch
42.	K — Q 4	R — Q 8 ch
43.	K — K 5	R — K 8 ch
44.	K — B 6	R — K R 8
45.	R — K 8 ch	K — R 2
46.	P — R 8 (Q)	R × Q
47.	R × R	K — Kt 3
48.	K × P	K × P
49.	K × P	K — B 4
50.	K — K 5	Resigns.

This ending shows how easy it is to make weak moves, and how often, even in master-play, mistakes are made and opportunities are lost. It shows that, so long as there is no great advantage of material, even with a good position, a player, no matter how strong, cannot afford to relax his attention even for one move.

27. THE DANGER OF A SAFE POSITION

Example 58. — A good proof of the previous statement is shown in the following ending between Marshall and Kupchick in one of their two games in the same Tournament (Havana, 1913).

It is evident that Marshall (White) is under great difficulties in the above position. Not only is he bound to lose a Pawn, but his position is rather poor. The best he could hope for was a draw unless something altogether unexpected happened, as it did. No reason can be given for Black's loss of the game except that he felt so certain of having the best of it with a Pawn more and what he considered a safe position, that he became exceedingly careless and did not consider the danger that actually existed. Let us see how it happened.

       1. P — Kt 4   R × R P

The mistakes begin. This is the first. Black sees that he can take a Pawn without any danger, and does not stop to think whether there is anything better. R — B 7 ch was the right move. If then K — Kt 3, R × P. If instead White played K — K 4, then R — K 4 ch followed by R × R P.

2. R — Q 1   R — R 5 ch

Mistake number two, and this time such a serious one as to almost lose the game. The proper move was to play P — B 4 in order to break up White's Pawns and at the same time make room for the Black King, which is actually in danger, as will soon be seen.

3. R — Q 4   R (R 5) — R 4

Mistake number three and this time fatal. His best move was R (Kt 4) — R 4. After the text move there is no defence. Black's game is lost. This shows that even an apparently simple ending has to be played with care. From a practically won position Black finds himself with a lost game, and it has only taken three moves.

4. R (Q 4) — Q 8   R — Kt 2

If 4...P — B 4; 5 R — R 8 ch, K — Kt 3; 6 R (B 8) — Kt 8 ch, K — B 3; 7 R × P ch, R — Kt 3; 8 P — Kt 5 ch, K — K 2; 9 R (R 6) × R, P × R; 10 R — Kt 7 ch, K — K 1; 11 R × Kt P, and wins easily.

5. P — R 4   P — R 4
6. R — R 8 ch   Resigns.

The reason is evident. If 6...K — Kt 3; 7 P × P ch,

R × P; 8 R × R, K × R; 9 R — R 8 ch, K — Kt 3;
10 P — R 5 mate.

28.   ENDINGS WITH ONE ROOK AND PAWNS

The reader has probably realised by this time that endings of two Rooks and Pawns are very difficult, and that the same holds true for endings of one Rook and Pawns. Endings of two Rooks and Pawns are not very common in actual play; but endings of one Rook and Pawns are about the most common sort of endings arising on the chess board. Yet though they do occur so often, few have mastered them thoroughly. They are often of a very difficult nature, and sometimes while apparently very simple they are in reality extremely intricate. Here is an example from a game between Marshall and Rosenthal in the Manhattan Chess Club Championship Tournament of 1909–1910.

Example 59.

In this position Marshall had a simple win by
R — B 7 ch, but played P — B 6, and thereby gave
Black a chance to draw. Luckily for him Black did
not see the drawing move, played poorly, and lost.
Had Black been up to the situation he would have
drawn by playing R — Q 3.

    1. P — B 6   R — Q 3 !

Now White has two continuations, either (*a*) P — B 7,
or (*b*) R — B 7 ch. We have therefore :

  (*a*) 2. P — B 7   R — Q 1 !
    3. R — R 5 ch K — B 5

and White will finally have to sacrifice the Rook for
Black's Pawn. Or —

  (*b*) 2. R — B 7 ch K — Q 5 !
    3. P — B 7   R — Kt 3 ch!

a very important move, as against R — K B 3, R — K 7
wins.

    4. K — B 1   R — K B 3
    5. R — Kt 7   K — B 6

and White will finally have to sacrifice the Rook
for the Pawn, or draw by perpetual check.

  If there were nothing more in the ending it would
not be of any great value, but there are other
very interesting features. Now suppose that after
1 P — B 6, R — Q 3; 2 P — B 7, Black did not
realise that R — Q 1 was the only move to draw,

We would then have the following position:

Now there would be two other moves to try: either (a) R — Kt 3 ch, or (b) R — K B 3. Let us examine them.

	(a) 1.	R — Kt 3 ch
	2. K — B 3	R — B 3 ch
	3. K — K 3	R — K 3 ch

If P — Kt 6; R — R 5 ch wins, because if the King goes back, then R — R 6, and if the King goes up, then R — R 4 ch, followed by R — K B 4 wins.

	4. K — Q 3	R — K B 3

If R — Q 3 ch; K — K 4 wins.

	5. R — R 5 ch	K moves
	6. R — R 6 wins	

	(b) 1.	R — B 3
	2. R — Kt 7 !	K — B 5

If P — Kt 6; R — Kt 3, and White will either capture the Pawn or go to K B 3, and come out with a winning ending.

3. P — R 4   P — Kt 6
4. R — Kt 4 ch   K moves
5. R — Kt 3

and White will either capture the Pawn or play R —
K B 3, according to the circumstances, and come out
with a winning ending.

Now, going back to the position shown on page 122,
suppose that after 1 P — B 6, R — Q 3; 2 R — B 7 ch,
Black did not realise that K — Q 5 was the only move
to draw, and consequently played K — Kt 3 instead,
we would then have the following position:

Now the best continuation would be:

1. P — B 7   R — Kt 3 ch (best)
2. K — B 1   R — K B 3
3. R — K 7 !   K — B 4 (best)

White threatened to check with the Rook at K 6.

4. K — K 2   P — Kt 6

Best. If K — B 5; both P — R 4 and K — K 3 will win; the last-named move particularly would win with ease.

5. R — K 3   P — Kt 7 (best)
6. R — Q Kt 3   R × P
7. R × P   R — K R 2
8. R — Q 2   R × P
9. K — K 3

This position we have arrived at is won by White, because there are two files between the opposing King and the Pawn from which the King is cut off by the Rook, and besides, the Pawn can advance to the fourth rank before the opponent's Rook can begin to check on the file. This last condition is very important, because if, instead of the position on the diagram, the Black Rook were at K R 1, and Black had the move, he could draw by preventing the advance of the Pawn, either through constant checks or by playing R — K B 1 at the proper time.

Now that we have explained the reasons why this position is won, we leave it to the student to work out the correct solution.

The fact that out of one apparently simple ending we have been able to work out several most unusual and difficult endings should be sufficient to impress upon the student's mind the necessity of becoming well acquainted with all kinds of endings, and especially with endings of Rook and Pawns.

29. A DIFFICULT ENDING: TWO ROOKS AND PAWNS

Following our idea that the best way to learn endings as well as openings is to study the games of the masters, we give two more endings of two Rooks and Pawns. These endings, as already stated, are not very common, and the author is fortunate in having himself played more of these endings than is generally the case. By carefully comparing and studying the endings already given (Examples 56 and 57) with the following, the student no doubt can obtain an idea of the proper method to be followed in such cases. The way of procedure is somewhat similar in all of them.

Example 60. — From a game, Capablanca-Kreymborg, in the New York State Championship Tournament of 1910.

It is Black's move, and no doubt thinking that drawing such a position (that was all Black played for) would be easy, he contented himself with a waiting policy. Such conduct must always be criticised. It often leads to disaster. *The best way to defend such positions is to assume the initiative and keep the opponent on the defensive.*

1. ....   Q R — K 1

The first move is already wrong. There is nothing to gain by this move. Black should play P — Q R 4; to be followed by P — Q R 5; unless White plays P — Q Kt 3. That would *fix* the Queen's side. After that he could decide what demonstration he could make with his Rooks to keep the opponent's Rooks at bay.

2. R — Q 4

This move not only prevents P — B 5 which Black intended, but threatens P — Kt 3, followed, after

P × P ch, by the attack with one or both Rooks against Black's Q R P.

$$2. \quad \ldots\ldots\ldots \quad R - B \, 3$$

probably with the idea of a demonstration on the King's side by R — Kt 3 and Kt 7.

$$3. \ P - Kt \, 3 \qquad P \times P \ ch$$
$$4. \ P \times P \qquad K - B \, 2$$
$$5. \ K - Q \, 3$$

R — Q R 1 should have been played now, in order to force Black to defend with R — K 2. White, however, does not want to disclose his plan at once, and thus awaken Black to the danger of his position, hence this move, which seems to aim at the disruption of Black's Queen's side Pawns.

$$5. \quad \ldots\ldots\ldots \quad R - K \, 2$$
$$6. \ R - Q R \, 1 \qquad K - K \, 3$$

This is a mistake. Black is unaware of the danger of his position. He should have played P — Kt 4; threatening R — R 3, and, by making this demonstration against White's K R P, stop the attack against his Queen's side Pawns, which will now develop.

$$7. \ R - R \, 6 \qquad R - Q B \, 2$$

He could not play K — Q 3, because P — Q B 4 would win at least a Pawn. This in itself condemns his last move K — K 3, which has done nothing but make his situation practically hopeless.

$$8. \ R \ (Q \, 4) - Q R \, 4 \quad P - K Kt \, 4$$

Now forced, but it is a little too late. He could not play 8...K R — B 2, because P — K B 4 would have left his game completely paralysed. Black now finally awakens to the danger, and tries to save the day by the counter-demonstration on the King's side, which he should have started before. Of course, White cannot play R × R P, because of R × R, followed by R — R 3, recovering the Pawn with advantage.

9. P — K R 4 !   P — Kt 5

Black is now in a very disagreeable position. If he played 9...P × P; 10 R × P would leave him in a very awkward situation, as he could not go back with the King, nor could he do much with either Rook. He practically would have to play 10...P — K R 3, when White would answer 11 P — Kt 4, threatening to win a Pawn by P — Kt 5, or, if that were not enough, he might play K — Q 4, to be followed finally by the entry of the King at B 5 or K 5.

10. K — K 2

10. .... P × P ch

Again he cannot play P — K R 4, because P — K B 4 would leave him paralysed. The advance of his K R P would make White's K R P safe, and consequently his K R would have to retire to K B 2 to defend the Q R P. That would make it impossible for his King to go to Q 2, because of the Q R P, nor could he advance a single one of his Pawns. On the other hand, White would play P — Kt 4, threatening to win a Pawn by P — Kt 5, or he might first play K — Q 4, and then at the proper time P — Kt 5, if there was nothing better. Black meanwhile could really do nothing but mark time with one of his Rooks. Compare this bottling-up system with the ending in Example 57, and it will be seen that it is very similar.

    11. K × P   R (B 3) — B 2
    12. K — K 2

Probably wrong. P — Kt 4 at once was the right move. The text move gives Black good chances of drawing.

    12. .... K — Q 3
    13. P — Kt 4   R — Q Kt 2

This could never have happened had White played 12 P — Kt 4, as he could have followed it up by P — Kt 5 after Black's K — Q 3.

    14. P — R 5

Not good. P — K B 4 offered the best chances of winning by force. If then 14...R — Kt 2; 15 P —

R 5, R — Kt 7 ch ; 16 K — Q 3, R — K R 7 ; 17 R × P, R × R ; 18 R × R, R × P ; 19 R — R 6, with winning chances.

14. ....   P — R 3

Black misses his last chance. P — B 5 would draw. If then 15 P × P, R (Kt 2) — K 2 ch! ; 16 K — B 1, R × P ; 17 R × P, R — K 6!

15.	P — K B 4	R — Kt 2
16.	K — Q 3	R (K Kt 2) — K 2
17.	R — R 1	R — Kt 2
18.	K — Q 4	R — Kt 7
19.	R (R 6) — R 2	R (Kt 2) — Kt 2

R (Kt 7) — Kt 2 would have offered greater resistance, but the position is lost in any case. (I leave the student to work this out.)

20.	K — Q 3 !	R × R
21.	R × R	R — K 2

Nothing would avail. If 21...R — Kt 8; 22 R — R 6! R — Q 8 ch; 23 K — B 2, R — K R 8; 24 P — Kt 5, R × P; 25 R × P ch, K — Q 2; 26 R — Q R 6, and White will win easily.

22.	R — K Kt 2	R — K 3
23.	R — Kt 7	R — K 2
24.	R — Kt 8	P — B 4

Black is desperate. He sees he can no longer defend his Pawns.

25.	R — Kt 6 ch	R — K 3
26.	P × P ch	K — Q 2
27.	R — Kt 7 ch	K — B 3
28.	R × P	K × P
29.	R — K B 7	Resigns.

Example 61. — From the game Capablanca-Janowski, New York National Tournament of 1913.

Black's game has the disadvantage of his double Q B P, which, to make matters worse, he cannot advance, because as soon as Black plays P — Q Kt 3, White replies P — Q Kt 4. It is on this fact that White builds his plans. He will stop Black's Queen's side Pawns from advancing, and will then bring his own King to K 3. Then in due time he will play P — Q 4, and finally P — K 5, or P — K Kt 5, thus forcing an exchange of Pawns and obtaining in that way a clear passed Pawn on the King's file. It will be seen that this plan was carried out during the course of the game, and that White obtained his winning advantage in that way. The play was based throughout on the chance of obtaining a passed Pawn on the King's file, with which White expected to win.

1. P — K Kt 4

already preparing to play P — K Kt 5 when the time comes.

1. ....   P — Q Kt 3

Black wants to play P — Q B 4, but White, of course, prevents it.

2. P — Kt 4 !   K — Kt 2

This King should come to the King's side, where the danger lurks.

3. K — B 2   P — Q Kt 4

With the object of playing K — Kt 3 and P — Q R 4, followed by P × P, and thus have an open file for his Rook and be able to make a counter-demonstration

on the Queen's side in order to stop White's advance
on the right.   White, however, also prevents this.

4. P — Q R 4 !   R — Q 5

Of course if P × P; Black will have all his Pawns on
the Queen's side disrupted and isolated, and White
can easily regain the lost Pawn by playing either
Rook on the Q R file.

5. R — Q Kt 1   R — K 4

He still wants to play P — Q B 4, but as it is easy
to foresee that White will again prevent it, the text
move is really a serious loss of time.   Black should
bring his King over to the other side immediately.

6. K — K 3   R — Q 2
7. P — R 5

The first part of White's strategic plan is now accomplished.   Black's Pawns on the Queen's side are *fixed*
for all practical purposes.

7. ....   R — K 3

If R × R; Kt P × R would have given White a very
powerful centre.   Yet it might have been the best
chance for Black.

8. R (Kt) — K B 1   R (Q 2) — K 2
9. P — Kt 5   P × P
10. R × P

The second part of White's strategical plan is now
accomplished. It remains to find out if the advantage
obtained is sufficient to win. White not only has a
passed Pawn, but his King is in a commanding position
in the centre of the board ready to support the advance
of White's Pawns, or, if necessary, to go to Q B 5, or
to move to the right wing in case of danger. Besides,
White holds the open file with one of his Rooks. Altogether White's position is superior and his chances
of winning are excellent.

10.	....	R — R 3
11.	R — Kt 3	R (R 3) — K 3

to prevent P — Q 4. Also Black fears to keep his
Rook in front of his two King's side Pawns which he
may want to utilise later.

12.	P — R 4	P — Kt 3
13.	R — Kt 5	P — R 3

White threatens P — R 5, which would finally force Black to take, and then White would double his Rooks against the isolated Pawn and win it, or tie up Black's Rooks completely. The text move, however, only helps White; therefore Black had nothing better than to hold tight and wait. R — K 4 would not help much, as White would simply answer R — B 8, R — K 1; R (Kt 5) × R, and whichever Rook Black took, White would have an easy game. (The student should carefully study these variations.)

14.	R — Kt 4	R — Kt 2
15.	P — Q 4	K — B 1
16.	R — B 8 ch	K — Kt 2

K — Q 2 would not help much, but since he made the previous move he should now be consistent and play it.

17.	P — K 5	P — Kt 4
18.	K — K 4	R (K 3) — K 2
19.	P × P	P × P
20.	R — B 5	K — B 1
21.	R (Kt 4) × P	R — R 2
22.	R — R 5	K — Q 2
23.	R × R	R × R
24.	R — B 8	R — R 5 ch
25.	K — Q 3	R — R 6 ch

26. K – Q 2   P – B 4
27. Kt P × P   R – Q R 6
28. P – Q 5   Resigns.

The winning tactics in all these endings have merely consisted in keeping the opponent's Rooks tied to the defence of one or more Pawns, leaving my own Rooks free for action. This is a general principle which can be equally applied to any part of the game. It means in general terms —

Keep freedom of manœuvre while hampering your opponent.

There is one more thing of great importance, and that is that the winning side has always had a general strategical plan capable of being carried out with the means at his disposal, while often the losing side had no plan at all, but simply moved according to the needs of the moment.

30. ROOK, BISHOP AND PAWNS v. ROOK, KNIGHT AND PAWNS

We shall now examine an ending of Rook, Bishop and Pawns against Rook, Knight and Pawns, where it will be seen that the Rook at times is used in the same way as in the endings already given.

Example 62. — From the first game of the Lasker-Marshall Championship Match in 1907.

In this position it is Black's move. To a beginner
the position may look like a draw, but the advanced
player will realise immediately that there are great
possibilities for Black to win, not only because he has
the initiative, but because of White's undeveloped
Queen's side and the fact that a Bishop in such a position is better than a Knight (see Section 14). It will
take some time for White to bring his Rook and Knight
into the fray, and Black can utilise it to obtain an
advantage. There are two courses open to him. The
most evident, and the one that most players would
take, is to advance the Pawn to Q B 4 and Q B 5
immediately in conjunction with the Bishop check
at R 3 and any other move that might be necessary
with the Black Rook. The other, and more subtle,
course was taken by Black. It consists in utilising
his Rook in the same way as shown in the previous
endings, forcing White to defend something all the
time, restricting the action of White's Knight and

White's Rook, while at the same time keeping freedom
of action for his own Rook and Bishop.

> 1. . . . .   R — Kt 1

This forces P — Q Kt 3, which blocks that square
for the White Knight.

> 2. P — Kt 3   R — Kt 4

bringing the Rook to attack the King's side Pawns
so as to force the King to that side to defend them,
and thus indirectly making more secure the position
of Black's Queen's side Pawns.

> 3. P — B 4   R — K R 4
> 4. K — Kt 1   P — B 4

Note that the White Knight's sphere of action is
very limited, and that after Kt — Q 2 White's own
Pawns are in his way.

> 5. Kt — Q 2   K — B 2
> 6. R — B 1 ch

This check accomplishes nothing. It merely drives
Black's King where it wants to go. Consequently
it is a very bad move. P — Q R 3 at once was the
best move.

> 6. . . . .   K — K 2
> 7. P — Q R 3   R — R 3

Getting ready to shift the attack to the Queen's side,
where he has the advantage in material and position.

> 8. P — K R 4   R — R 3

Notice how similar are the manœuvres with this Rook to those seen in the previous endings.

        9. R — R 1   B — Kt 5

Paralysing the action of the Knight and *fixing* the whole King's side.

      10. K — B 2   K — K 3

White cannot answer Kt — B 3, because B × Kt followed by K — K 4 will win a Pawn, on account of the check at K B 3 which cannot be stopped.

      11. P — R 4   K — K 4
      12. K — Kt 2   R — K B 3
      13. R — K 1   P — Q 6
      14. R — K B 1   K — Q 5

Now the King attacks White's Pawns and all will soon be over.

      15. R × R   P × R
       6. K — B 2   P — B 3

Merely to exhaust White's move, which will finally force him to move either the King or the Knight.

      17. P — Q R 5   P — Q R 3
      18. Kt — B 1   K × P
      19. K — K 1   B — K 7
      20. Kt — Q 2 ch   K — K 6
      21. Kt — Kt 1   P — B 4
      22. Kt — Q 2   P — R 4
      23. Kt — Kt 1   K — B 6
      24. Kt — B 3   K × P

25.	Kt — R 4	P — B 5
26.	Kt × P	P — B 6
27.	Kt — K 4 ch	K — B 5

The quickest way to win. White should resign.

28.	Kt — Q 6	P — B 4
29.	P — Kt 4	P × P
30.	P — B 5	P — Kt 6
31.	Kt — B 4	K — Kt 6
32.	Kt — K 3	P — Kt 7
	Resigns.	

A very good example on Black's part of how to conduct such an ending.

CHAPTER VI

FURTHER OPENINGS AND MIDDLE-GAMES

31. SOME SALIENT POINTS ABOUT PAWNS

BEFORE going back to the discussion of openings and middle-game positions, it might be well to bear in mind a few facts concerning Pawn positions which will no doubt help to understand certain moves, and sometimes even the object of certain variations in the openings, and of some manœuvres in the middle-games.

Example 63. — In the position of the diagram we have an exceedingly bad Pawn formation on Black's side. Black's Q B P is altogether backward, and White could by means of the open file concentrate

his forces against that weak point. There is also the square at White's Q B 5, which is controlled by White, and from where a White piece once established could not be dislodged. In order to get rid of it, Black would have to exchange it, which is not always an easy matter, and often when possible not at all convenient. The same holds true with regard to Black's K P, K B P and K Kt P, which create what is called a "hole" at Black's K B 3. Such Pawn formations invariably lead to disaster, and consequently must be avoided.

Example 64. — In this position we might say that the White centre Pawns have the attacking position, while the Black centre Pawns have the defensive position. Such a formation of Pawn occurs in the French Defence. In such positions White most often attempts, by means of P — K B 4 and K B 5, to obtain a crushing attack against Black's King, which is generally Castled on the King's side. To prevent that,

and also to assume the initiative or obtain material advantage, Black makes a counter-demonstration by P — Q B 4, followed by P × P (when White defends the Pawn by P — Q B 3), and the concentrating of Black's pieces against the White Pawn at Q 4. This in substance might be said to be a determined attack against White's centre in order to paralyse the direct attack of White against Black's King. It must be remembered that at the beginning of the book it was stated that *control of the centre was an essential condition to a successful attack against the King.*

In an abstract way we may say that two or more Pawns are strongest when they are in the same rank next to one another. Thus the centre Pawns are strongest in themselves, so to speak, when placed at K 4 and Q 4 respectively, hence the question of advancing either the one or the other to the fifth rank is one that must be most carefully considered. The advance of either Pawn often determines the course the game will follow.

Another thing to be considered is the matter of one or more passed Pawns when they are isolated either singly or in pairs. We might say that a passed Pawn is either very weak or very strong, and that its weakness or strength, whichever happens to be in the case to be considered, increases as it advances, and is at the same time in direct relation to the number of pieces on the board. In this last respect it might be generally said that *a passed Pawn increases in strength as the number of pieces on the board diminishes.*

Having all this clear in mind we will now **revert** to the openings and middle-game. We will analyse games carefully from beginning to end according to general principles. I shall, whenever possible, use my own games, not because they will better illustrate the point, but because, knowing them thoroughly, I shall be able to explain them more authoritatively than the games of others.

32. SOME POSSIBLE DEVELOPMENTS FROM A RUY LOPEZ

That some of the variations in the openings and the manœuvres in the middle-game are often based on some of the elementary principles just expounded can be easily seen in the following case:

Example 65.

1.	P — K 4	P — K 4
2.	Kt — K B 3	Kt — Q B 3
3.	B — Kt 5	P — Q R 3
4.	B — R 4	Kt — B 3
5.	O — O	Kt × P
6.	P — Q 4	P — Q Kt 4
7.	B — Kt 3	P — Q 4
8.	P × P	B — K 3
9.	P — B 3	B — K 2
10.	R — K 1	Kt — B 4
11.	B — B 2	B — Kt 5
12.	Q Kt — Q 2	O — O
13.	Kt — Kt 3	Kt — K 3

So far a very well-known variation of the Ruy Lopez. In fact, they are the moves of the Janowski-Lasker game in Paris, 1912.

14. Q — Q 3   P — Kt 3

Let us suppose the game went on, and that in some way White, by playing one of the Knights to Q 4 at the proper time, forced the exchange of both Knights, and then afterwards both the Bishops were exchanged, and we arrived at some such position as shown in the following diagram. (I obtained such a position in a very similar way once at Lodz in Poland. I was playing the White pieces against a consulting team headed by Salwe.)

Now we would have here the case of the backward Q B P, which will in no way be able to advance to Q B 4. Such a position may be said to be theoretically lost, and in practice a first-class master will invariably win it from Black. (If I may be excused the reference, I will say that I won the game above referred to.)

After a few moves the position may be easily thus:

The Black pieces can be said to be *fixed*. If White plays Q — Q B 3, Black must answer Q — Q 2, otherwise he will lose a Pawn, and if White returns with the Queen to Q R 3 Black will have again to return to Q Kt 2 with the Queen or lose a Pawn. Thus Black can only move according to White's lead, and under such conditions White can easily advance with his Pawns to K B 4 and K Kt 4, until Black will be forced to stop P — B 5 by playing P — K B 4, and we might finally have some such position as this:

Example 66.

In this situation the game might go on as follows:

1. P × P, P × P; 2. Q — K B 3, Q — Q 2

White threatened to win a Pawn by Q × P, and Black could not play 2...R — K B 1, because 3 R × B P would also win a Pawn at least.

3. R (B 5) — B 2, R — Kt 3;   4. R — Kt 2, K — R 1;
5. R (B 1) — K Kt 1,   R (B 1) — K Kt 1;
6. Q — R 5, R × R;   7. R × R, R × R;
8. K × R, Q — Kt 2 ch;   9. K — R 2, Q — Kt 3;
10. Q × Q, P × Q;   11. P — Kt 4, and White wins.

Now suppose that in the position in the preceding diagram it were Black's move, and he played R — K B 1. White would then simply defend his K B P by some move like Q — K B 3, threatening R × Q B P, and then he would bring his King up to Kt 3, and when the time came, break through, as in the previous case. White might even be able to obtain the following position:

Black would now be forced to play R — B 1, and White could then play Q — B 2, and follow it up with K B 3, and thus force Black to play P × P, which would give White a greater advantage.

A careful examination of all these positions will reveal that, besides the advantage of freedom of manœuvre on White's part, the power of the Pawn at K 5 is enormous, and that it is the commanding position of this Pawn, and the fact that it is free to advance, once all the pieces are exchanged, that constitute the pivot of all White's manœuvres.

I have purposely given positions without the moves which lead to them so that the student may become accustomed to build up in his own mind possible positions that may arise (out of any given situation). Thus he will learn to make strategical plans and be on his way to the master class. The student can derive enormous benefit by further practice of this kind.

33. THE INFLUENCE OF A "HOLE"

The influence of a so-called "hole" in a game has already been illustrated in my game against Blanco (page 81), where has been shown the influence exercised by the different pieces posted in the hole created at White's K 5.

Example 67. — In order to further illustrate this point, I now give a game played in the Havana International Masters Tournament of 1913. (Queen's Gambit Declined.) White: D. Janowski. Black: A. Kupchick.

1.	P — Q 4	P — Q 4
2.	P — Q B 4	P — K 3
3.	Kt — Q B 3	Kt — K B 3
4.	B — Kt 5	B — K 2
5.	P — K 3	Q Kt — Q 2
6.	B — Q 3	P × P
7.	B × P	Kt — Kt 3

Of course the idea is to post a Knight at Q 4, but as it is the other Knight which will be posted there this manœuvre does not seem logical. The Knight at Kt 3 does nothing except to prevent the development of his own Q B. The normal course O — O, followed by P — Q B 4, is more reasonable. For a beautiful illustration of how to play White in that variation, see the Janowski-Rubinstein game of the St. Petersburg Tournament of 1914.

8. B — Q 3

B — Kt 3 has some points in its favour in this position, the most important being the possibility of advancing the King's Pawn immediately after 8...K Kt — Q 4; 9 B × B, Q × B.

8.	....	K Kt — Q 4
9.	B × B	Q × B
10.	Kt — B 3	

Had White's Bishop been at Q Kt 3 he could now play P — K 4 as indicated in the previous note, a move which he cannot make in the present position, because of Kt — K B 5 threatening, not only the K Kt P, but also Kt × B ch. As White's King's Bishop should never be exchanged in this opening without a very good reason White therefore cannot play P — K 4.

> 10. ....   O — O
> 11. O — O   B — Q 2
> 12. R — B 1

White is perfectly developed, and now threatens to win a Pawn as follows: Kt × Kt, Kt × Kt; P — K 4, followed by R × P.

> 12. ....   P — Q B 3

The fact that Black is practically forced to make this move in order to avoid the loss of a Pawn is sufficient reason in itself to condemn the whole system of development on Black's part. In effect, he plays B — Q 2, and now he has to shut off the action of his own Bishop, which thereby becomes little more than a Pawn for a while. In fact, it is hard to see how this Bishop will ever be able to attack anything. Besides, it can be easily seen that White will soon post his two Knights at K 5 and Q B 5 respectively, and that Black will not be able to dislodge them without seriously weakening his game, if he can do it at all. From all these reasons it can be gathered that it would probably have been better for Black to play Kt × Kt and thus get rid of one of the two White Knights before assuming such a defensive position. In such cases, the less the number of pieces on the board, the better chances there are to escape.

13. Kt — K 4   P — K B 4

This practically amounts to committing suicide, since it creates a hole at K 5 for White's Knight, from where it will be practically impossible to dislodge him. If Black intended to make such a move he should have done it before, when at least there would have been an object in preventing the White Knight from reaching B 5.

14. Kt — B 5   B — K 1
15. Kt — K 5

The position of White's Knights, especially the one at K 5, might be said to be ideal, and a single glance shows how they dominate the position. The question henceforth will be how is White going to derive the full benefit from such an advantageous situation. This we shall soon see.

15. ....   R — Kt 1

There is no object in this move, unless it is to be followed by Kt — Q 2. As that is not the case, he might have gone with the Rook to B 1, as he does later.

16.	R — K 1	R — B 3
17.	Q — B 3	R — R 3
18.	Q — Kt 3	R — B 1

White threatened to win the exchange by playing either Kt — B 7 or Kt — Kt 4.

19.	P — B 3	R — B 2
20.	P — Q R 3	K — R 1
21.	P — R 3	

Perhaps all these precautions are unnecessary, but White feels that he has more than enough time to prepare his attack, and wants to be secure in every way before he begins.

21.	. . . .	P — Kt 4
22.	P — K 4	P — B 5
23.	Q — B 2	Kt — K 6

He had better have played Kt — B 3; and tried later on to get rid of White's Knights by means of Kt — Q 2.

24. R × Kt

with this sacrifice of the Rook for a Knight and Pawn White obtains an overwhelming position.

| 24. | . . . . | P × R |
| 25. | Q × P | Kt — B 1 |

Kt — Q 2 was better in order to get rid of one of the two White Knights. There were, however, any number of good replies to it, among them the following: Kt (B 5) × Kt, B × Kt; Q × P, Q × Q; Kt — B 7 ch, K — Kt 2; Kt × Q, and with two Pawns for the exchange, and the position so much in his favour, White should have no trouble in winning.

26.	Kt — Kt 4	R — Kt 3
27.	P — K 5	R — Kt 2
28.	B — B 4	B — B 2

All these moves are practically forced, and as it is
easily seen they tie up Black's position more and
more. White's manœuvres from move 24 onwards
are highly instructive.

29.	Kt — B 6	Kt — Kt 3

This wandering Knight has done nothing throughout
the game.

30.	Kt (B 5) — K 4	P — K R 3
31.	P — K R 4	Kt — Q 4
32.	Q — Q 2	R — Kt 3
33.	P × P	Q — B 1

If P × P; K — B 2, and Black would be helpless.

34.	P — B 4	Kt — K 2
35.	P — K Kt 4	P × P
36.	P × P	Resigns.

There is nothing to be done. If B — Kt 1; Q — R 2 ch,
K — Kt 2; B × P.

The student should notice that, apart from other
things, White throughout the game has had control
of the Black squares, principally those at K 5 and
Q B 5.

From now on to the end of the book I shall give a
collection of my games both lost and won, chosen so
as to serve as illustrations of the general principles
laid down in the foregoing pages.

PART II

PART II

GAME 1. QUEEN'S GAMBIT DECLINED
(Match, 1909)

White: F. J. Marshall. Black: J. R. Capablanca.

1.	P — Q 4	P — Q 4
2.	P — Q B 4	P — K 3
3.	Kt — Q B 3	Kt — K B 3
4.	B — Kt 5	B — K 2
5.	P — K 3	Kt — K 5

I had played this defence twice before in the match with good results, and although I lost this game I still played it until the very last game, when I changed my tactics. The reason was my total lack of knowledge of the different variations in this opening, coupled with the fact that I knew that Dr. E. Lasker had been successful with it against Marshall himself in 1907. I thought that since Dr. Lasker had played it so often, it should be good. The object is to exchange a couple of pieces and at the same time to bring about a position full of possibilities and with promising chances of success once the end-game stage is reached. On general principles it should be wrong, because the same Knight is moved three times in the opening, although it involves the exchange of two pieces. In reality the difficulty in this variation, as well as in nearly all the variations of the Queen's gambit, lies in the slow development of Black's Queen Bishop. However, whether this variation can or cannot be safely played is a question still to be decided, and it is outside the scope of this book. I may add that at present my preference is for a different system of development, but it is not unlikely that I should some time come back to this variation.

6. B × B   Q × B
7. B — Q 3

P × P is preferable for reasons that we shall soon see.

7. ....   Kt × Kt
8. P × Kt   Kt — Q 2

Now P × P would be a better way to develop the game. The idea is that after 8...P × P; 9 B × B P, P — Q Kt 3, followed by B — Kt 2, would give Black's Bishop a powerful range. For this variation see the eleventh game of the match.

9. Kt — B 3   O — O

No longer would 9...P × P; 10 B × B P, P — Q Kt 3 be good, because 11 B — Kt 5 would prevent B — Kt 2 on account of Kt — K 5.

10.	P × P	P × P
11.	Q — Kt 3	Kt — B 3
12.	P — Q R 4	P — B 4

Played with the intention of obtaining the majority of Pawns on the Queen's side. Yet it is doubtful whether this move is good, since it leaves Black's Queen's-side Pawns disrupted in a way. The safer course would have been to play P — B 3.

13.	Q — R 3	P — Q Kt 3

This exposes Black to further attack by P — R 5 without any compensation for it. If I had to play this position nowadays I would simply play 13... R — K 1. Then after 14 Q × P, Q × Q would follow, and I believe that Black would regain the Pawn. If, instead, White played 14 P × P then B — Kt 5 would give Black an excellent game.

14.	P — R 5	B — Kt 2
15.	O — O	Q — B 2
16.	K R — Kt 1	Kt — Q 2

Black's position was bad and perhaps lost in any case, but the text move makes matters worse. As a matter of fact I never saw White's reply B — B 5. It never even passed through my mind that this was threatened. Black's best move would have been 16...K R — Kt 1. If that loses, then any other move would lose as well.

| 17. | B — B 5 | K R — B 1 |

From bad to worse. Kt — B 3 offered the only hope.

18.	B × Kt	Q × B
19.	P — R 6	B — B 3
20.	P × P	P × P
21.	Q × P	Q R — Kt 1

The game was lost. One move was as good as another.

22.	R × R	R × R
23.	Kt — K 5	Q — B 4
24.	P — K B 4	R — Kt 3
25.	Q × R !	Resigns.

Of course, if 25 Kt × B, R — Kt 8 ch would have drawn. The text move is pretty and finishes quickly. A well-played game on Marshall's part.

GAME 2. QUEEN'S GAMBIT DECLINED

(San Sebastian, 1911)

White: A. K. Rubinstein.   Black: J. R. Capablanca.

1.	P — Q 4	P — Q 4
2.	Kt — K B 3	P — Q B 4
3.	P — B 4	P — K 3
4.	P × Q P	K P × P
5.	Kt — B 3	Kt — Q B 3
6.	P — K Kt 3	B — K 3

Kt — B 3 is the normal move in this variation. White's development was first introduced by Schlechter and elaborated later on by Rubinstein. It aims at the isolation of Black's Q P, against which the White pieces are gradually concentrated. In making the text move I was trying to avoid the beaten track. Being a developing move there should be no objection to it in the way of general principles, except that the Knights ought to come out before the Bishops.

7.	B — Kt 2	B — K 2
8.	O — O	R — B 1

In pursuance of the idea of changing the normal

course of this variation, but with very poor success. The move in theory ought to be unsound, since Black's K Kt is yet undeveloped. I had not yet learned of the attack founded on Kt — Kt 5 and the exchange of the B at K 3. Either Kt — B 3 or P — K R 3; to prevent either B or Kt — K Kt 5, was right.

	9.	P × P	B × P
	10.	Kt — K Kt 5	Kt — B 3
	11.	Kt × B	P × Kt
	12.	B — R 3	Q — K 2
	13.	B — Kt 5	O — O

This is a mistake. The right move was R — Q 1 in order to get the Rook away from the line of the Bishop at R 3 and at the same time to support the Q P. Incidentally it shows that White failed to take proper advantage of Black's weak opening moves. Against the text move White makes a very fine combination which I had seen, but which I thought could be defeated.

14. B × Kt   Q × B

I considered P × B, which it seemed would give me a playable game, but I thought White's combination unsound and therefore let him play it, to my lasting regret.

15. Kt × P!   Q—R 3

16. K — Kt 2 !

This is the move which I had not considered. I thought that Rubinstein would have to play B — Kt 2, when I had in mind the following winning combination: 16 B — Kt 2, Kt — K 4! 17 Kt — B 4 (if R — B 1, Q × R !! Q × Q, B × P ch wins), Kt — Kt 5; 18 P — K R 3 (if Kt — R 3, B × P ch wins the exchange), Kt × P; 19 R × Kt, B × R ch; 20 K × B, P — K Kt 4, and Black should win. It is curious that this combination has been overlooked. It has been taken for granted that I did not see the 17th move Q — B 1.

16. .... Q R — Q 1

After White's last move there was nothing for me to do but submit to the inevitable.

17.	Q — B 1 !	P × Kt
18.	Q × B	Q — Q 7
19.	Q — Kt 5	Kt — Q 5
20.	Q — Q 3	Q × Q
21.	P × Q	K R — K 1
22.	B — Kt 4	

This gives Black a chance. He should have played K R — K 1. If then Kt — B 7; R × R ch, R × R; R — Q B 1, R — K 7; K — B 1, Kt — Q 5 (if R — Q 7; B — K 6 ch, K — B 1; B × P would win); R — B 8 ch, K — B 2; R — B 7 ch, R — K 2; R — B 5 wins.

22.	....	R — Q 3
23.	K R — K 1	R × R
24.	R × R	R — Q Kt 3
25.	R — K 5	R × P
26.	R × P	Kt — B 3
27.	B — K 6 ch	K — B 1
28.	R — B 5 ch	K — K 1
29.	B — B 7 ch	K — Q 2
30.	B — B 4	

| 30. | .... | P — Q R 3 |

A bad move, which gives away any legitimate chance Black had to draw. It loses a very important move. In fact, as the course of the game will show, it loses several moves. The proper way was to play K — Q 3. If then R — Q Kt 5, R × R; B × R, Kt — Q 5; followed by P — Q Kt 4; and White would have an exceedingly difficult game to draw on account of the dominating position of the Knight at

Q 5 in conjunction with the extra Pawn on the Queen's side and the awkward position of White's King. (See how this is so.)

31.	R — B 7 ch	K — Q 3
32.	R × K Kt P	P — Kt 4
33.	B — Kt 8	P — Q R 4
34.	R × P	P — R 5
35.	P — R 4	P — Kt 5
36.	R — R 6 ch	K — B 4
37.	R — R 5 ch	K — Kt 3
38.	B — Q 5	

With these last three moves White again gives Black a chance. Even before the last move B — B 4 would have won with comparative ease, but the text move is a downright blunder, of which, fortunately for him, Black does not avail himself.

38. .... P — Kt 6

R × P would make it practically impossible for White to win, if he can win at all. White's best con-

tinuation then would have been : 39 B — B 4, R — B 7;
40 R — Kt 5 ch, K — B 2 ; 41 B — Kt 8, P — R 6;
42 P — R 5, P — R 7; 43 B × P, R × B, and if there
is a win it is very difficult to find it, as against
44 P — R 6, R — R 3 ! offers excellent chances for a
draw.

39.	P × P	P — R 6
40.	B × Kt	R × Kt P

If 40...P — R 7; 41 R — Kt 5 ch, K — R 3;
42 R — Kt 8.

41.	B — Q 5	P — R 7
42.	R — R 6 ch	Resigns.

As an end game, this is rather a sad exhibition for
two masters. The redeeming feature of the game is
Rubinstein's fine combination in the middle game,
beginning with 14 B × Kt.

GAME 3.   IRREGULAR DEFENCE
(Havana, 1913)

White : D. Janowski.   Black : J. R. Capablanca.

1.	P — Q 4	Kt — K B 3
2.	Kt — K B 3	P — Q 3
3.	B — Kt 5	Q Kt — Q 2
4.	P — K 3	P — K 4
5.	Kt — B 3	P — B 3
6.	B — Q 3	B — K 2
7.	Q — K 2	Q — R 4
8.	O — O	Kt — B 1
9.	K R — Q 1	B — Kt 5

At last Black is on his way to obtain full development. The idea of this irregular opening is mainly
to throw White on his own resources. At the time
the game was played, the system of defence was not
as well known as the regular forms of the Queen's
Pawn openings. Whether it is sound or not remains
yet to be proved. Its good features are that it keeps
the centre intact without creating any particular weakness, and that it gives plenty of opportunity for deep
and concealed manœuvring. The drawback is the
long time it takes Black to develop his game. It is
natural to suppose that White will employ that time
to prepare a well-conceived attack, or that he will use
the advantage of his development actually to prevent
Black's complete development, or failing that, to
obtain some definite material advantage.

10.	P — K R 3	B — R 4
11.	P × P	P × P
12.	Kt — K 4	

12. .... Kt × Kt

A very serious mistake. I considered castling, which was the right move, but desisted because I was afraid that by playing 13 B × Kt, P × B; 14 Kt — Kt 3, B — Kt 3; 15 Kt — B 5, White would obtain a winning position for the end game. Whether right or wrong this shows how closely related are all parts of the game, and consequently how one will influence the other.

13.	B × B	K × B
14.	B × Kt	B — Kt 3

Not good. The natural and proper move would have been Kt — K 3, in order to bring all the Black pieces into play. B × Kt at once was also good, as it would have relieved the pressure against Black's King's Pawn, and at the same time have simplified the game.

Here it is seen how failure to comply with the elementary logical reasons, that govern any given position, often brings the player into trouble. I was no doubt influenced in my choice of moves by the fear of B — B 5, which was a very threatening move.

15.	Q — B 4	Kt — K 3
16.	P — Q Kt 4	Q — B 2
17.	B × B	R P × B
18.	Q — K 4	K — B 3

19. R — Q 3

P — K R 4, to be followed by P — Kt 4, might have
been a more vigorous way to carry on the attack.
Black's weak point is unquestionably the Pawn at
K 4, which he is compelled to defend with the King.
The text move aims at doubling the Rooks, with the
ultimate object of placing one of them at Q 6, supported by a Pawn at Q B 5, Black could only stop
this by playing P — B 4, which would create a "hole"
at Q 5; or by playing P — Kt 3, which would tie the
Black Queen to the defence of the Q B P as well as
the K P, which she already defends. Black, however, can meet all this by offering the exchange of
Rooks, which destroys White's plans. For this reason
P — K R 4 appears the proper way to carry on the
attack.

19. .... Q R — Q 1
20. Q R — Q 1 P — K Kt 4

This move is preparatory to P — K Kt 3, which would

make Black's position secure. Unfortunately for Black, he did not carry out his original plan.

21. P—B 4   R × R

P—K Kt 3 would have left Black with a perfectly safe game.

22. R × R   R—Q 1

A very serious mistake, which loses a Pawn. P—K Kt 3 was the right move, and would have left Black with a very good game. In fact, if it should come to a simple ending, the position of the Black King would be an advantage.

23. R × R   Kt × R

24. P—K R 4

This wins a Pawn, as will soon be seen. Black cannot reply 24...Kt—K 3; because 25 P × P ch, Kt × P; 26 Q—R 4 wins the Knight.

24.	. . . .	P × P
25.	Q × P ch	K — K 3
26.	Q — Kt 4 ch	K — B 3
27.	Q — Kt 5 ch	K — K 3
28.	Q × P	Q — Q 3
29.	P — B 5	Q — Q 4
30.	P — K 4 !	Q — Q 8 ch
31.	K — R 2	P — B 3
32.	Q — Kt 4 ch !	K — K 2
33.	Kt × P	Q × Q
34.	Kt × Q	Kt — K 3
35.	P — K 5	P × P
36.	Kt × P	Kt — Q 5

The game went on for a few more moves, and, there being no way to counteract the advance of White's two passed Pawns, Black resigned.

GAME 4.   FRENCH DEFENCE

(St. Petersburg, 1913)

White: J. R. Capablanca.   Black: E. A. Snosko-Borovski.

1.	P — Q 4	P — K 3
2.	P — K 4	P — Q 4
3.	Kt — Q B 3	Kt — K B 3
4.	B — Kt 5	B — Kt 5

This constitutes the *McCutcheon Variation*. It aims at taking the initiative away from White. Instead of defending, Black makes a counter demonstration on the Queen's side. It leads to highly interesting games.

5. P × P

At the time this game was played the variation 5 P — K 5 was in vogue, but I considered then, as I do now, the text move to be the stronger.

5. .... Q × P

This is considered superior to P × P. It has for its object, as I said before, to take the initiative away from White by disrupting White's Queen's side. White, however, has more than ample compensation through his breaking up Black's King's side. It might be laid down as a principle of the opening that *the breaking up of the King's side is of more importance than a similar occurrence on the Queen's side.*

6. B × Kt	B × Kt ch
7. P × B	P × B
8. Kt — B 3	P — Q Kt 3

The plan of Black in this variation is to post his Bishop on the long diagonal so as to be able later on, in conjunction with the action of his Rooks along the open K Kt's file, to make a violent attack against White's King. It is, of course, expected that White will Castle on the King's side because of the broken-up condition of his Queen's side Pawns.

	9. Q—Q 2	B—Kt 2
	10. B—K 2	Kt—Q 2
	11. P—B 4	Q—K B 4
	12. O—O—O	

An original idea, I believe, played for the first time in a similar position in a game against Mr. Walter Penn Shipley, of Philadelphia. My idea is that as there is no Black Bishop and because Black's pieces have been developed with a view to an attack on the King's side, it will be impossible for Black to take advantage of the apparently unprotected position of White's King. Two possibilities must be considered. Firstly: If Black Castles on the Queen's side, as in this game, it is evident that there is no danger of an attack. Secondly: If Black Castles on the King's side, White begins the attack first, taking advantage of the awkward position of Black's Queen. In addition to the attacking probabilities of the text move, White in one move brings his King into safety and brings one of his Rooks into play. Thus he gains several moves, "tempi" as they are called, which will serve him to develop whatever plan he may wish to evolve.

	12.	O—O—O
	13. Q—K 3	K R—Kt 1
	14. P—Kt 3	Q—Q R 4

Unquestionably a mistake, overlooking White's fine

reply, but a careful examination will show that White already has the better position.

15. R — Q 3 !   K — Kt 1
16. K R — Q 1   Q — K B 4

17. Kt — R 4

This move has been criticised because it puts the Knight out of the way for a few moves. But by forcing Q — K Kt 4 ; White gains a very important move with P — B 4, which not only consolidates his position, but also drives the Queen away, putting it out of the game for the moment. Certainly the Queen is far more valuable than the Knight, to say nothing of the time gained and the freedom of action obtained thereby for White's more important pieces.

17. . . . .   Q — K Kt 4
18. P — B 4   Q — Kt 2
19. B — B 3

In such positions it is generally very advantageous to get rid of the Black Bishop controlling his Q R 3 and Q B 3, which form "holes" for White's pieces. The Bishop in such positions is of very great defensive value, hence the advantage of getting rid of it.

19.	....	K R — K 1
20.	B × B	K × B
21.	P — Q B 5 !	P — B 3

White threatened P — B 6 ch.

| 22. | Kt — B 3 | Q — B 1 |

To prevent the Knight from moving to Q 6 via Q 2 and K 4 or Q B 4. It is self-evident that White has a great advantage of position.

23. Kt — Q 2 ?

I had considered R — Kt 3, which was the right move, but gave it up because it seemed too slow, and that in such a position there had to be some quicker way of winning.

| 23. | .... | P × P |
| 24. | Kt — B 4 | |

Kt — K 4 or Kt — Kt 3 would have brought about an ending advantageous to White.

24.	....	Kt — Kt 3
25.	Kt — R 5 ch	K — R 1
26.	P × P	Kt — Q 4
27.	Q — Q 4	R — B 1

If R — Kt 1; 28 Kt × P, R (Kt 1) — B 1; 29 Kt × P would win.

28. P — B 4

Kt — B 4 was the right move. I was, however, still looking for the "grand combination," and thought that the Pawn I would later on have at Q 6 would win the game. Black deserves great credit for the way in which he conducted this exceedingly difficult defence. He could easily have gone wrong any number of times, but from move 22 onwards he always played the best move.

28.	....	P — K 4 !
29.	Q — Kt 1	P — K 5
30.	P × Kt	P × R
31.	P — Q 6	R — K 7
32.	P — Q 7	R — B 7 ch
33.	K — Kt 1	R — Kt 1 ch
34.	Kt — Kt 3	Q — K 2

35. R × P

The position is most interesting. I believe I lost here my last chance to win the game, and if that is true it would vindicate my judgment when, on move 28, I played P — B 4. The student can find out what would happen if White plays Q — Q 4 ! at once. I have gone over the following variations : 35 Q — Q 4, R × K R P (of course if R × B P, P — Q 8 wins);

36 Q × Q P! R — Q 1; 37 Q — R 6, K — Kt 1 best
(if Q — Q 5 ch; K — R 1, K — Kt 1; R — Q Kt 1 wins);
38 Q × B P and White will at least have a draw.

35.	....	R — K 7
36.	Q — Q 4	R — Q 1
37.	Q — R 4	Q — K 5
38.	Q — R 6	K — Kt 1

There is nothing to be done against this simple move,
since White cannot play Kt — Q 4, because Q — R 8
mates.

39.	K — B 1	R × Q P
40.	Kt — Q 4	R — K 8 ch
	Resigns.	

A very interesting battle.

GAME 5. RUY LOPEZ

(St. Petersburg, 1914)

White: Dr. E. Lasker. Black: J. R. Capablanca.

1.	P — K 4	P — K 4
2.	Kt — K B 3	Kt — Q B 3
3.	B — Kt 5	P — Q R 3
4.	B × Kt	

The object of this move is to bring about speedily
a middle-game without Queens, in which White

has four Pawns to three on the King's side, while Black's superiority of Pawns on the other side is somewhat balanced by the fact that one of Black's Pawns is doubled. On the other hand, Black has the advantage of remaining with two Bishops while White has only one.

4.	....	Q P × B
5.	P — Q 4	P × P
6.	Q × P	Q × Q
7.	Kt × Q	B — Q 3

Black's idea is to Castle on the King's side. His reason is that the King ought to remain on the weaker side to oppose later the advance of White's Pawns. Theoretically there is very much to be said in favour of this reasoning, but whether in practice that would be the best system would be rather difficult to prove. The student should notice that if now all the pieces were exchanged White would practically be a Pawn ahead, and would therefore have a won ending.

8. Kt — Q B 3   Kt — K 2

A perfectly sound form of development. In any other form adopted the Black Kt could not be developed either as quickly or as well. K 2 is the natural position for the Black Kt in this variation, in order not to obstruct Black's Pawns, and also, in some eventualities, in order to go to K Kt 3. There is also the possibility of its going to Q 5 via Q B 3 after P — Q B 4.

9. O — O   O — O

10. P — B 4

This move I considered weak at the time, and I do still. It leaves the K P weak, unless it advances to K 5, and it also makes it possible for Black to pin the Kt by B — Q B 4.

10. ....   R — K 1

Best. It threatens B — B 4; B — K 3, Kt — Q 4. It also prevents B — K 3 because of Kt — Q 4 or B 4.

11. Kt — Kt 3   P — B 3

Preparatory to P — Q Kt 3, followed by P — Q B 4 and B — Kt 2 in conjunction with Kt — Kt 3, which would put White in great difficulties to meet the combined attack against the two centre Pawns.

12. P — B 5

It has been wrongly claimed that this wins the game, but I would like nothing better than to have such a position again. It required several mistakes on my part finally to obtain a lost position.

12. ....   P — Q Kt 3
13. B — B 4

13. ....   B — Kt 2

Played against my better judgment. The right move of course was B × B. Dr. Lasker gives the following variation: 13...B × B; 14 R × B, P — B 4; 15 Q R — Q 1, B — Kt 2; 16 R — B 2, Q R — Q 1; 17 R × R, R × R; 18 R — Q 2, R × R; 19 Kt × R, and he claims that White has the best of it. But, as Niemzovitch pointed out immediately after the game, 16...Q R — Q 1 given in Dr. Lasker's variation, is not the best. If 16...Q R — B 1! then White will have great difficulty in drawing the game,

since there is no good way to stop Black from playing
Kt — B 3, followed by Kt — K 4, threatening Kt —
B 5. And should White attempt to meet this ma-
nœuvre by withdrawing the Kt at Kt 3; then the
Black Knight can go to Q 5, and the White Pawn at
K 4 will be the object of the attack. Taking Dr.
Lasker's variation, however, whatever advantage there
might be disappears at once if Black plays 19...Kt —
B 3, threatening Kt — Kt 5 and also Kt — Q 5, neither
of which can be stopped. If White answers 20 Kt —
Q 5, Kt — Q 5 for Black will at least draw. In fact,
after 19...Kt — B 3 Black threatens so many things
that it is difficult to see how White can prevent the
loss of one or more Pawns.

$$14. \ B \times B \qquad P \times B$$
$$15. \ Kt — Q 4$$

It is a curious but true fact that I did not see this
move when I played 13...B — Kt 2, otherwise I would
have played the right move 13...B × B.

$$15. \ \ldots\ldots\ldots \qquad Q R — Q 1$$

The game is yet far from lost, as against the entry
of the Knight, Black can later on play P — B 4, followed by P — Q 4.

$$16. \ Kt — K 6 \qquad R — Q 2$$
$$17. \ Q R — Q 5$$

I now was on the point of playing P — B 4, to be
followed by P — Q 4, which I thought would give me
a draw, but suddenly I became ambitious and thought
that I could play the text move, 17...Kt — B 1,
and later on sacrifice the exchange for the Knight
at K 6, winning a Pawn for it, and leaving White's
K P still weaker. I intended to carry this plan either
before or after playing P — K Kt 4 as the circumstances
demanded. Now let us analyse: 17...P — B 4. If
18 Kt — Q 5, B × Kt; 19 P × B, P — Q Kt 4; and a
careful analysis will show that Black has nothing to
fear. Black's plan in this case would be to work his
Kt around to K 4, via Q B 1, Q Kt 3, and Q B 5 or
Q 2. Again, 17...P — B 4; 18 R — B 2, P — Q 4;
19 P × P, B × P; 20 Kt × B (best, since if R (B 2) —
Q 2, B × Kt give Black the advantage), R × Kt;
21 R × R, Kt × R; and there is no good reason why
Black should lose.

17. .... Kt — B 1
18. R — B 2 P — Q Kt 4

19.	K R — Q 2	R (Q 2) — K 2
20.	P — Q Kt 4	K — B 2
21.	P — Q R 3	B — R 1

Once more changing my plan and this time without any good reason. Had I now played R × Kt; P × R ch, R × P; as I intended to do when I went back with the Knight to B 1, I doubt very much if White would have been able to win the game. At least it would have been extremely difficult.

22.	K — B 2	R — R 2
23.	P — Kt 4	P — R 3
24.	R — Q 3	P — Q R 4
25.	P — K R 4	P × P
26.	P × P	R (R 2) — K 2

This, of course, has no object now. Black, with a bad game, flounders around for a move. It would have been better to play R — R 6 to keep the open file, and at the same time to threaten to come out with the Knight at Kt 3 and B 5.

| 27. | K — B 3 | R — Kt 1 |
| 28. | K — B 4 | P — Kt 3 |

Again bad. White's last two moves were weak, since the White King does nothing here. He should have played his Rook to Kt 3 on the 27th move. Black now should have played P — Kt 4 ch. After missing this chance White has it all his own way, and finishes the game most accurately, and Black becomes more helpless with each move. The game needs no further comment, excepting that my play throughout was of an altogether irresolute character. When a plan is made, it must be carried out if at all possible. Regarding the play of White, I consider his 10th and 12th moves were very weak; he played well after that up to the 27th move, which was bad, as well as his 28th move. The rest of his play was good, probably perfect.

29.	R — Kt 3	P — Kt 4 ch
30.	K — B 3	Kt — Kt 3
31.	P × P	R P × P
32.	R — R 3	R — Q 2
33.	K — Kt 3 !	K — K 1
34.	Q R — K R 1	B — Kt 2
35.	P — K 5	Q P × P
36.	Kt — K 4	Kt — Q 4
37.	Kt (K 6) — B 5	B — B 1
38.	Kt × R	B × Kt
39.	R — R 7	R — B 1
40.	R — R 1	K — Q 1
41.	R — R 8 ch	B — B 1
42.	Kt — B 5	Resigns.

GAME 6. FRENCH DEFENCE

(Rice Memorial Tournament, 1916)

White: O. Chajes.   Black: J. R. Capablanca.

1.	P — K 4	P — K 3
2.	P — Q 4	P — Q 4
3.	Kt — Q B 3	Kt — K B 3
4.	B — Kt 5	B — Kt 5

Of all the variations of the French Defence I like this best, because it gives Black more chances to obtain the initiative.

5. P — K 5

Though I consider P × P the best move, there is much to be said in favour of this move, but not of the variation as a whole, which White adopted in this game.

5.	.. ..	P — K R 3
6.	B — Q 2	B × Kt
7.	P × B	Kt — K 5
8.	Q — Kt 4	K — B 1

The alternative, P — K Kt 3; leaves Black's King's side very weak. White by playing P — K R 4 would force Black to play P — K R 4; and later, on White's Bishop by going to Q 3, would threaten the weakened K Kt P. By the text move Black gives up Castling, but gains time for an attack against White's centre and Queen's side.

9. B — B 1   P — Q B 4

Threatening Q — R 4 and stopping thereby **White's** threat of B — R 3. It demonstrates that White's last move was a complete loss of time and merely weakened his position.

10.	B — Q 3	Q — R 4
11.	Kt — K 2	P × P
12.	O — O	P × P
13.	B × Kt	P × B
14.	Q × P	Kt — B 3

Black has come out of the opening with a Pawn to the good. His development, however, has suffered somewhat, and there are Bishops of opposite colour, so that it cannot be said as yet, that Black has a won game; but he has certainly the best of the position, because, besides being a Pawn to the good, he **threatens** White's K P, which must of course be defended, and this in turn will give him the opportunity to post his Knight at Q 4 via K 2. When the Black Knight is posted at Q 4, the Bishop will be developed to B 3 via Q 2, as soon as the opportunity presents itself, and it will be Black that will then have the initiative, and can consequently decide the course of the game.

15. R — Q 1

To prevent Kt — K 2; which would be answered by Kt × P, or still better by B — R 3. The move, however, is strategically wrong, since by bringing his pieces to the Queen's side, White loses any chance he might have of making a determined attack on the King's side before Black is thoroughly prepared for it.

15. . . . .   P — K Kt 3
16. P — B 4   K — Kt 2
17. B — K 3

Better would have been P — Q R 4, in order to play B — R 3. The White B would be much better posted on the open diagonal than here, where it acts purely on the defensive.

17. . . . .   Kt — K 2
18. B — B 2   Kt — Q 4

This Knight completely paralyses the attack, as it dominates the whole situation, and there is no way to dislodge it. Behind it Black can quietly develop his pieces. The game can now be said to be won for Black strategically.

19. R — Q 3	B — Q 2
20. Kt — Q 4	Q R — Q B 1
21. R — Kt 3	K — R 2
22. P — K R 4	K R — Kt 1
23. P — R 5	Q — Kt 5

In order to pin the Knight and be ready to come back to either K 2 or B 1. Also to prevent Q R — Kt 1. In reality nearly all these precautions are unnecessary, since White's attack amounts to nothing. Probably Black should have left aside all these considerations, and played Q — R 5 now, in order to follow it up with P — B 4, as he did later, but under less favourable circumstances.

24. R — R 3

24. ....   P — B 4

Not the best, as White will soon prove. Q — B 1 would have avoided everything, but Black wants to assume the initiative at once and plunges into com-

plications. However, as will soon be seen, the move
is not a losing one by any means.

> 25. P × P e.p.   Kt × P (B 3)
> 26. P × P ch   R × P

> 27. R × P ch

This wins the Queen.

> 27. ....   K × R
> 28. Kt — B 5 ch   P × Kt
> 29. Q × Q

The position looks most interesting. I thought it would be possible to get up such an attack against the White King as to make it impossible for him to hold out much longer, but I was wrong, unless it could have been done by playing B — B 3 first, forcing P — Kt 3 and then playing K — R 4. I followed a similar plan, but lost a very important move by playing Q R — K Kt 1; which gave White time to play R — Q 1. I am convinced, however, that B — B 3 at once was the right move. White would be forced to play P — Kt 3, and Black would reply with either K — R 4; as already indicated, which looks the best (the plan, of course, is to play R — K R 1; and follow it up with K — Kt 5; threatening mate, or some other move according to circumstances. In some cases, of course, it will be better first to play K — Kt 5), or Kt — K 5, which will at least give him a draw. There are so many possibilities in this position that it would be impossible to give them all. It will be worth the reader's time to go carefully through the lines of play indicated above.

29. .... Q R — K Kt 1

As stated B — B 3 was the best move.

30. P — Kt 3   B — B 3
31. R — Q 1   K — R 4

The plan, of course, as explained above, is to go to Kt 5 in due time and threaten mate at K R 8, but it is now too late, the White Rook having come in time to prevent the manœuvre. Instead of the text move, therefore, Black should have played Kt — K 5; which would have given him a draw at the very least. After the text moves the tables are turned. It is now White who has the upper hand, and Black who has to fight for a draw.

	32.	R — Q 6	B — K 5

Kt — K 5 was still the right move, and probably the last chance Black had to draw against White's best play.

33.	Q × B P	Kt — Q 4
34.	R × R	K × R

Kt × Q; R × R, Kt × P was no better.

35.	Q — K 5	K — B 2
36.	P — B 4	R — K 1
37.	Q — Kt 2	Kt — B 3
38.	B — Q 4	R — K R 1
39.	Q — Kt 5	R — R 8 ch
40.	K — B 2	P — R 3
41.	Q — Kt 6	R — R 7 ch
42.	K — K 1	Kt — Q 2
43.	Q — Q 6	B — B 3
44.	P — Kt 4	P × P
45.	P — K B 5	R — R 8 ch
46.	K — Q 2	K — K 1
47.	P — B 6	R — R 2
48.	Q — K 6 ch	K — B 1
49.	B — K 3	R — B 2
50.	B — R 6 ch	K — Kt 1

Most players will be wondering, as the spectators did, why I did not resign. The reason is that while I knew the game to be lost, I was hoping for the following variation, which Chajes came very near playing: 51 Q × P ch, K — R 2; 52 Q — R 5, R × P; 53 B — Kt 5 ch, K — Kt 2; 54 B × R ch, K × B; and while White has a won game it is by no means easy. If the reader does not believe it, let him take the White pieces against a master and see what happens. My opponent, who decided to take no chances, played 51 B — Kt 7, and finally won as shown below.

51.	B — Kt 7	P — Kt 6
52.	K — K 2	P — Kt 7
53.	K — B 2	Kt — B 1
54.	Q — Kt 4	Kt — Q 2
55.	K — Kt 1	P — R 4
56.	P — R 4	B × P
57.	Q — R 3	R × P
58.	B × R	Kt × B
59.	Q × P ch	K — B 1
60.	Q × P	

and after a very few more moves Black resigned.

A very fine game on Chajes' part from move 25 on, for while Black, having the best of the position, missed several chances, White, on the other hand, missed none.

GAME 7. RUY LOPEZ

(San Sebastian, 1911)

White : J. R. Capablanca.   Black : A. Burn

1.	P — K 4	P — K 4
2.	Kt — K B 3	Kt — Q B 3
3.	B — Kt 5	P — Q R 3
4.	B — R 4	Kt — B 3
5.	P — Q 3	

This is a very solid development, to which I was much addicted at the time, because of my ignorance of the multiple variations of the openings.

5.	....	P — Q 3
6.	P — B 3	B — K 2

In this variation there is the alternative of developing this Bishop via Kt 2, after P — K Kt 3.

7.	Q Kt — Q 2	O — O
8.	Kt — B 1	P — Q Kt 4
9.	B — B 2	P — Q 4
10.	Q — K 2	P × P
11.	P × P	B — Q B 4

Evidently to make room for the Queen at K 2, but I do not think the move advisable at this stage. B — K 3 is a more natural and effective move. It develops a piece and threatens B — B 5, which would have to be stopped.

12.	B — Kt 5	B — K 3

Now it is not so effective, because White's Q B is out, and the Knight, in going to K 3 to defend the square Q B 4, does not block the Q B.

13. Kt — K 3   R — K 1
14. O — O   Q — K 2

This is bad. Black's game was already not good. He probably had no choice but to take the Knight with the Bishop before making this move.

15. Kt — Q 5   B × Kt
16. P × B   Kt — Kt 1

in order to bring it to Q 2, to support the other Knight and also his King's Pawn. White, however, does not allow time for this, and by taking advantage of his superior position is able to win a Pawn.

17. P — Q R 4   P — Kt 5

Since he had no way to prevent the loss of a Pawn, he should have given it up where it is, and played Q Kt — Q 2, in order to make his position more solid.

The text move not only loses a Pawn, but leaves Black's game very much weakened.

18.	P × P	B × P
19.	B × Kt	Q × B
20.	Q — K 4	B — Q 3
21.	Q × P ch	K — B 1

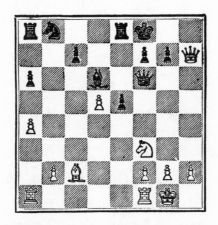

With a Pawn more and all his pieces ready for action, while Black is still backward in development, it only remains for White to drive home his advantage before Black can come out with his pieces, in which case, by using the open K R file, Black might be able to start a strong attack against White's King. White is able by his next move to eliminate all danger.

22.	Kt — R 4	Q — R 3

This is practically forced. Black could not play P — Kt 3 because of B × P, and White meanwhile threatened Q — R 8 ch followed by Kt — B 5 ch and Q × P.

23.	Q × Q	P × Q
24.	Kt — B 5	P — K R 4
25.	B — Q 1	Kt — Q 2
26.	B × P	Kt — B 3
27.	B — K 2	Kt × P
28.	K R — Q 1	Kt — B 5
29.	B — B 4	K R — Q 1
30.	P — R 4	P — R 4

Black must lose time assuring the safety of this Pawn.

31.	P — K Kt 3	Kt — K 3
32.	B × Kt	P × B
33.	Kt — K 3	K R — Kt 1
34.	Kt — B 4	K — K 2

Black fights a hopeless battle. He is two Pawns down
for all practical purposes, and the Pawns he has are
isolated and have to be defended by pieces.

35.	Q R — B 1	R — R 2

White threatened Kt × B, followed by R — B 7 ch.

36.	R — K 1	K — B 3
37.	R — K 4	R — Kt 5
38.	P — Kt 4	R — R 3

If R × R P; Kt × B of course would win a piece

39.	R — B 3	B — B 4
40.	R — B 3 ch	K — Kt 2
41.	P — Kt 3	B — Q 5
42.	K — Kt 2	R — R 1

43. P — Kt 5	R — R 3
44. P — R 5	R × Kt
45. P × R	R — B 3
46. P — Kt 6	Resigns.

GAME 8. CENTRE GAME

(Berlin, 1913)

White : J. Mieses.   Black : J. R. Capablanca.

1. P — K 4	P — K 4
2. P — Q 4	P × P
3. Q × P	Kt — Q B 3
4. Q — K 3	Kt — B 3
5. Kt — Q B 3	B — Kt 5
6. B — Q 2	O — O
7. O — O — O	R — K 1

In this position, instead of the text move, P — Q 3 is often played in order to develop the Q B. My idea was to exert sufficient pressure against the K P to win it, and thus gain a material advantage, which would, at least, compensate whatever slight advantage of position White might have. The plan, I think, is quite feasible, my subsequent difficulties being due to faulty execution of the plan.

8. Q — Kt 3	Kt × P
9. Kt × Kt	R × Kt
10. B — K B 4	

10. .... Q — B 3

White's threat to regain the Pawn was merely with the idea of gaining time to develop his pieces. Black could have played P — Q 3; opening the way for his Q B, when would have followed, 11 B — Q 3, R — K 1; 12 Kt — B 3, and White would soon start a powerful direct attack against Black's King. With the text move Black aims at taking the initiative away from White in accordance with the principles laid down in this book.

11. Kt — R 3

If B × P, P — Q 3; and White's Bishop would be completely shut off, and could only be extricated, if at all, with serious loss of position. The text move aims at quick development to keep the initiative.

11. .... P — Q 3

This now is not only a developing move, but it also threatens to win a piece by B × Kt.

12. B — Q 3   Kt — Q 5

This complicates the game unnecessarily. R — K 1;
was simple, and perfectly safe.

13. B — K 3

13. .... B — Kt 5

This is a serious mistake. The position was most
interesting, and though in appearance dangerous for
Black, not so in reality. The right move would have
been 13...R — Kt 5, when we would have 14 B × Kt,
R × B; 15 P — Q B 3, B × P; 16 P × B, R — K Kt 5;
17 Q — K 3 (best), Q × P ch; 18 B — B 2, Q × Q;
19 P × Q, R × P, and Black has the best of the game
with four Pawns for a Knight, besides the fact that
all the White Pawns are isolated.

14. Kt — Kt 5 !   R × B

There was nothing better.

15. Q × B !   Kt — K 7 ch

16.	B × Kt !	R × B
17.	Kt — K 4 !	R × Kt
18.	Q × R	Q — Kt 4 ch
19.	P — K B 4	Q — Kt 4
20.	P — B 3	B — B 4
21.	K R — K 1	Q — B 3
22.	R — Q 5	

Q × Q would have given White a decided advantage, enough to win with proper play. Mieses, however, feared the difficulties of an ending where, while having the exchange, he would be a Pawn minus. He preferred to keep the Queens on the board and keep up the attack. At first sight, and even after careful thought, there seems to be no objection to his plan; but in truth such is not the case. From this point the game will gradually improve in Black's favour until, with the exchange ahead, White is lost.

22.	....	Q — Q 2
23.	P — B 5	P — Q B 3
24.	R — Q 2	P — Q 4

My plan for the moment is very simple. It will consist in bringing my Bishop around to B 3. Then I shall try to paralyse White's attack against my King by playing P — K R 3, and also prevent White from ever playing P — K Kt 5. Once my King is safe from attack I shall begin to advance my Queen's side Pawns, where there are four to three; and that advantage, coupled with the enormous attacking power of my Bishop at B 3, will at least assure me an even chance of success.

25.	Q — B 3	B — K 2
26.	Q R — K 2	B — B 3
27.	Q — R 5	P — K R 3
28.	P — K Kt 4	K — R 2 !

To prevent P — K R 4, which I would answer with
P — K Kt 3, winning the Queen. It can now be
considered that my King is safe from attack. White
will have to withdraw his Queen via R 3, and Black
can use the time to begin his advance on the Queen's
side.

    29. K — Kt 1   R — Q 1
    30. R — Q 1   P — B 4

Notice that, on assuming the defensive, White has
placed his Rooks correctly from the point of view of
strategy. They are both on white squares free from
the possible attack of the Black Bishop.

    31. Q — R 3   Q — R 5

This gains time by attacking the Rook and holding
the White Q at R 3 for the moment, on account of
the K Kt P. Besides, the Queen must be in the middle
of the fray now that the attack has to be brought
home. White has actually more value in material,
and therefore Black must utilise everything at his
command in order to succeed.

    32. R (K 2) — Q 2   Q — K 5 ch
    33. K — R 1   P — Q Kt 4

threatening P — Kt 5; which would open the line
of action of the Bishop and also secure a passed Pawn.

    34. Q — Kt 2   Q — R 5

indirectly defending the Q P, which White cannot
take on account of Q × R ch.

35. K—Kt 1	P—Kt 5

The attack increases in force as it is gradually brought home directly against the King. The position now is most interesting and extremely difficult. It is doubtful if there is any valid defence against Black's best play. The variations are numerous and difficult.

36. P × P	Q × P

Black has now a passed Pawn, and his Bishop exerts great pressure. White cannot very well play now 37 R × P because of R × R; 38 R × R, B × P; and White could not take the Bishop because Q—K 5 ch would win the Rook, leaving Black a clear passed Pawn ahead.

37. P—Q R 3	Q—R 5 !
38. R × P	R—Q Kt 1
39. R (Q 1)—Q 2	P—B 5
40. Q—Kt 3	R—Kt 6
41. Q—Q 6	

41. ....   P — B 6

B × P would also win, which shows that White's
game is altogether gone. In these cases, however,
it is not the prettiest move that should be played,
but the most effective one, the move that will make
your opponent resign soonest.

42. R — Q B 2   P × P
43. R — Q 3   Q — K 5 !
44. R — Q 1   R — Q B 6
    Resigns.

Of course White must play Q — Q 2, and Black then
plays R × P.

GAME 9.   QUEEN'S GAMBIT DECLINED

(Berlin, 1913)

White: J. R. Capablanca.   Black: R. Teichmann.

	White	Black
1.	P — Q 4	P — Q 4
2.	Kt — K B 3	Kt — K B 3
3.	P — B 4	P — K 3
4.	B — Kt 5	B — K 2
5.	Kt — B 3	Q Kt — Q 2
6.	P — K 3	O — O
7.	R — B 1	P — Q Kt 3
8.	P × P	P × P
9.	B — Kt 5	

An invention of my own, I believe. I played it on the spur of the moment simply to change the normal course of the game. Generally the Bishop goes to Q 3, or to R 6, after Q — R 4. The text move is in the nature of an ordinary developing move, and as it violates no principle it cannot be bad.

	White	Black
9.	....	B — Kt 2
10.	O — O	P — Q R 3
11.	B — R 4	R — B 1
12.	Q — K 2	P — B 4
13.	P × P	Kt × P

If P × P; K R — Q 1, and White would play to win one of Black's centre Pawns. The drawback to the text move is that it leaves Black's Q P isolated, and consequently weak and subject to attack.

14. K R — Q 1   Kt × B

The alternative would have been 14...P — Kt 4; 15 B — B 2, P — Kt 5; 16 Kt — Q R 4, Kt (B 4) — K 5.

15. Kt × Kt   P — Kt 4
16. R × R   Q × R
17. Kt — B 3   Q — B 5

Black aims at the exchange of Queens in order to remain with two Bishops for the ending, but in this position such a course is a mistake, because the Bishop at Kt 2 is inactive and cannot come into the game by any means, unless Black gives up the isolated Queen's Pawn which the Bishop must defend.

18. Kt — Q 4

Not, of course, R — Q 4, because of Q × Q; Kt × Q, R — B 1; and there would be no good way to prevent R — B 7.

18. ....   Q × Q
19. Kt (B 3) × Q !

Notice the co-ordination of the Knights' moves. They are manœuvred chain-like, so to speak, in order to maintain one of them, either at Q 4 or ready to go there. Now White threatens to take the open file, and therefore forces Black's next move.

19. ....   R — B 1

The student should examine this position carefully. There seems to be no particular danger, yet, as White will demonstrate, Black may be said to be lost. If the game is not altogether lost, the defence is at least of the most difficult kind; indeed, I must confess that I can see no adequate defence against White's next move.

       20. Kt — B 5 !   K — B 1

If 20...B — Q 1; 21 Kt — Q 6, R — B 2; 22 Kt × B, R × Kt; 23 B × Kt, B × B; 24 R × P, R — B 2; 25 R — Q 2, and White is a Pawn ahead. If 20...B moves anywhere else, then B × Kt, doubling the K B P and isolating all of Black's King's side Pawns.

       21. Kt × B   K × Kt
       22. Kt — Q 4   P — Kt 3

This is practically forced, as White threatened Kt — B 5 ch. Notice that the Black Knight is pinned in such a way that no relief can be afforded except by giving up the K R P or abandoning the open file with the Rook, which would be disastrous, as White would immediately sieze it.

23. P — B 3 !

23. ··········   P — R 3

Black could do nothing else except mark time with his Rook along the open file, since as soon as he moved away White would take it. White, on the other hand, threatens to march up with his King to K 5 via K B 2, K Kt 3, K B 4, after having, of course, prepared the way. Hence, Black's best chance was to give up a Pawn, as in the text, in order to free his Knight.

24. B × P   Kt — Q 2
25. P — K R 4   Kt — B 4
26. B — B 4   Kt — K 3

Black exchanges Knights to remain with Bishops of

opposite colours, which gives him the best chance to draw.

27. Kt × Kt   K × Kt

27...P × Kt would be worse, as White would then be able to post his Bishop at K 5.

28. R — Q 2   R — K R 1

Black wants to force B — Kt 3. P — K Kt 3 would be bad, on account of P — Q 5; which would get the Black Bishop into the game, even though White could answer P — K 4. The text move is, however, weak, as will soon be seen. His best chance was to play P — Kt 5; and follow it up with P — R 4 and B — R 3. White meanwhile could play P — Kt 4 and R 5, obtaining a passed Pawn, which, with proper play, should win.

29. R — Q B 2!   R — Q B 1
30. R × R   B × R

There are now Bishops of opposite colour, but nevertheless White has an easily-won game.

31. K — B 2

31. ....   P — Q 5

Practically forced. Otherwise the White King would
march up to Q 4 and then to B 5 and win Black's
Queen's side Pawns. If Black attempted to stop
this by putting his King at Q B 3 then the White King
would enter through K 5 into Black's King's side
and win just as easily.

32.	P × P	K — Q 4
33.	K — K 3	B — K 3
34.	K — Q 3	K — B 3
35.	P — Q R 3	B — B 5 ch
36.	K — K 3	B — K 3
37.	B — R 6	

It is better not to hurry P — K Kt 4 because of P — B 4 ;
for although White could win in any case, it would
take longer. Now the White King threatens to help
by going in through K B 4 after posting the Bishop

at Kt 7, where it not only protects the Q P, but indirectly also the Q Kt P.

37.	K — Q 4
38. B — Kt 7	Resigns.

The student ought to have realised by this time the enormous importance of playing well every kind of ending. In this game again, practically from the opening, White aimed at nothing but the isolation of Black's Q P. Once he obtained that, he tried for and obtained, fortunately, another advantage of position elsewhere which translated itself into the material advantage of a Pawn. Then by accurate playing in the ending he gradually forced home his advantage. This ending has the merit of having been played against one of the finest players in the world.

GAME 10. PETROFF DEFENCE

(St. Petersburg, 1914)

White: **J. R. Capablanca.**   Black: **F. J. Marshall.**

1.	P — K 4	P — K 4
2.	Kt — K B 3	Kt — K B 3
3.	Kt × P	P — Q 3
4.	Kt — K B 3	Kt × P
5.	Q — K 2	Q — K 2
6.	P — Q 3	Kt — K B 3
7.	B — Kt 5	

Played by Morphy, and a very fine move. The point is that should Black exchange Queens he will be a move behind in development and consequently will get a cramped game if White plays accurately.

7. ....   B — K 3

Marshall thought at the time that this was the best move and consequently played it in preference to Q × Q ch.

8.	Kt — B 3	P — K R 3
9.	B × Kt	Q × B
10.	P — Q 4	B — K 2
11.	Q — Kt 5 ch	Kt — Q 2
12.	B — Q 3 !	

It is now time to examine the result of the opening. On White's side we find the minor pieces well posted and the Queen out in a somewhat odd place, it is true, but safe from attack and actually attacking a Pawn.

White is also ready to Castle. White's position is evidently free from danger and his pieces can easily manœuvre.

On Black's side the first thing we notice is that he has retained both his Bishops, unquestionably an advantage; but on the other hand we find his pieces bunched together too much, and the Queen in danger of being attacked without having any good square to go to. The Bishop at K 2 has no freedom and it blocks the Queen, which, in its turn, blocks the Bishop. Besides, Black cannot Castle on the King's side because Q × P, R — Kt 1; Q — K 4 threatening mate, wins a Pawn. Nor can he Castle on the Queen's side because Q — R 5 would put Black's game in imminent danger, since he cannot play P — R 3 because of B × P; nor can he play K — Kt 1 because of Kt — Kt 5. Consequently we must conclude that the opening is all in White's favour.

12. . . . .   P — Kt 4

To make room for his Queen, threatening also P — Kt 5.

13. P — K R 3   O — O

giving up a Pawn in an attempt to free his game and take the initiative. It was difficult for him to find a move, as White threatened Kt — K 4, and should Black go with the Queen to Kt 2, then P — Q 5, B — B 4; Kt × P ch, followed by B × B.

14.	Q × P	Q R — Kt 1
15.	Q — K 4	Q — Kt 2
16.	P — Q Kt 3	P — Q B 4

In order to break up White's centre and bring his Knight to B 4 and thus lay the foundation for a violent attack against White's King. The plan, however, fails, as it always must in such cases, because Black's development is backward, and consequently his pieces are not properly placed.

| 17. | O — O | P × P |
| 18. | Kt — Q 5 ! |

A simple move, which destroys Black's plan utterly. Black will now have no concerted action of his pieces, and, as his Pawns are all weak, he will sooner or later lose them.

18.	....	B — Q 1
19.	B — B 4	Kt — B 4
20.	Q × P	Q × Q

The fact that he has to exchange Queens when he is a Pawn behind shows that Black's game is lost.

21.	Kt × Q	B × Kt
22.	B × B	B — B 3
23.	Q R — Q 1	B × Kt

The Knight was too threatening. But now the ending brought about is one in which the Bishop is stronger than the Knight; which makes Black's plight a desperate one. The game has no further interest, and it is only because of its value as a study of this variation of the Petroff that I have given it. Black was able to fight it out until the sixtieth move on account of some poor play on White's part. The rest of the moves are given merely as a matter of form.

24.	R × B	K — Kt 2
25.	B — B 4	R — Kt 3
26.	R — K 1	K — B 3
27.	P — B 4	Kt — K 3
28.	P × P ch	P × P
29.	R — B 1 ch	K — K 2
30.	R — Kt 4	R — K Kt 1
31.	R — B 5	R — B 3
32.	P — K R 4	K R — Q B 1
33.	P × P	R — B 4
34.	B × Kt	P × B
35.	R × R	R × R
36.	P — Kt 6	K — B 1
37.	R — Q B 4	R — Q R 4

38.	P — R 4	K — Kt 2
39.	R — B 6	R — Q 4
40.	R — B 7 ch	K × P
41.	R × P	R — Q 8 ch
42.	K — R 2	P — Q 4
43.	P — R 5	R — Q B 8
44.	R — B 7	R — Q R 8
45.	P — Q Kt 4	R — R 5
46.	P — B 3	P — Q 5
47.	R — B 6	P × P
48.	R × P	R × Kt P
49.	R — Q R 3	R — Kt 2
50.	P — R 6	R — Q R 2
51.	R — R 5	K — B 3
52.	P — Kt 4	K — K 2
53.	K — Kt 3	K — Q 3
54.	K — B 4	K — B 2
55.	K — K 5	K — Q 2
56.	P — Kt 5	K — K 2
57.	P — Kt 6	K — B 1
58.	K × P	K — K 1
59.	P — Kt 7	R × P
60.	P — R 7	R — Kt 3 ch
61.	K — B 5	Resigns.

GAME 11. RUY LOPEZ

(St. Petersburg, 1914)

White: J. R. Capablanca.   Black: D. Janowski.

1.	P — K 4	P — K 4
2.	Kt — K B 3	Kt — Q B 3
3.	B — Kt 5	P — Q R 3
4.	B × Kt	Q P × B
5.	Kt — B 3	

I played this move after having discussed it with Alechin on several occasions. Alechin considered it, at the time, superior to P — Q 4, which is generally played. He played it himself later on in the Tournament, in one of his games against Dr. E. Lasker, and obtained the superior game, which he only lost through a blunder.

| 5. | . . . . | B — Q B 4 |

P — B 3 is probably the best move in this position. I do not like the text move.

| 6. | P — Q 3 | B — K Kt 5 |
| 7. | B — K 3 | B × B |

This opens the K B file for White, and also reinforces his centre, but Black naturally did not want to make a second move with this Bishop.

| 8. | P × B | Q — K 2 |
| 9. | O — O | O — O — O |

Bold play, typical of Janowski.

10. Q — K 1   Kt — R 3

The problem for White now is to advance his Q Kt P to Kt 5 as fast as he can. If he plays P — Q Kt 4 at once, Black simply takes it. If he plays first P — Q R 3 and then P — Q Kt 4, he will still have to protect his Q Kt P before he can go on and play P — Q R 4 and P — Kt 5. As a matter of fact White played a rather unusual move, but one which, under the circumstances, was the best, since after it he could at once play P — Q Kt 4 and then P — Q R 4 and P — Kt 5.

11. R — Kt 1 !   P — B 3
12. P — Kt 4   Kt — B 2
13. P — Q R 4   B × Kt

He simplifies, hoping to lighten White's attack, which will have to be conducted practically with only the heavy pieces on the board. He may have also done it in order to play Kt — Kt 4 and K 3.

14. R × B

Taking with the Pawn would have opened a possibility for a counter attack.

14. .... P — Q Kt 3

He is forced to this in order to avoid the breaking up of his Queen's side Pawns. The only alternative would have been P — Q Kt 4; which on the face of it looks bad.

15. P — Kt 5   B P × P
16. P × P   P — Q R 4
17. Kt — Q 5   Q — B 4
18. P — B 4

The White Knight is now a tower of strength. Behind it White will be able to prepare an attack, which will begin with P — Q 4, to drive away the Black Queen and thus leave himself free to play P — B 5. There is only one thing to take care of and that is to prevent Black from sacrificing the Rook for the Knight and a Pawn.

18.	....	Kt — Kt 4
19.	R — B 2	Kt — K 3
20.	Q — B 3	R — Q 2

Had White on his 19th move played K R — B 1 instead of R — B 2, Black could have played now instead of the text move, R × Kt; K P × R, Q × P ch; followed by Kt — B 4 with a winning game.

21.	R — Q 1	K — Kt 2

It would have been better for Black to play K — Q 1. The text move loses very rapidly.

22.	P — Q 4	Q — Q 3
23.	R — B 2	P × P
24.	P × P	Kt — B 5
25.	P — B 5	Kt × Kt
26.	P × Kt	Q × Q P
27.	P — B 6 ch	K — Kt 1
28.	P × R	Q × P (Q 2)
29.	P — Q 5	R — K 1
30.	P — Q 6	P × P
31.	Q — B 6	Resigns.

GAME 12. FRENCH DEFENCE

(New York, 1918)

White: J. R. Capablanca.   Black: O. Chajes.

1.	P — K 4	P — K 3
2.	P — Q 4	P — Q 4
3.	Kt — Q B 3	Kt — K B 3
4.	B — Q 3	

Not the most favoured move, but a perfectly natural developing one, and consequently it cannot be bad.

4.	....	P × P

P — Q B 4 is generally played in this case instead of the text move.

5.	Kt × P	Q Kt — Q 2
6.	Kt × Kt ch	Kt × Kt
7.	Kt — B 3	B — K 2

8. Q — K 2

This is played to prevent P — Q Kt 3, followed by B — Kt 2, which is the general form of development for Black in this variation. If Black now plays 8 ... P — Q Kt 3; 9 B — Kt 5 ch, B — Q 2; 10 Kt — K 5 and White obtains a considerable advantage in position.

8. .... O — O
9. B — K Kt 5 P — K R 3

Of course Black could not play P — Q Kt 3 because of B × Kt, followed by Q — K 4.

10. B × Kt B × B
11. Q — K 4 P — K Kt 3

This weakens Black's King's side. R — K 1 was the right move.

12. P — K R 4

12. .... P — K 4

This is merely giving up a Pawn in order to come out quickly with his Q B. But as he does not obtain any compensation for his Pawn, the move is bad. He should have played Q — Q 4 and tried to fight the game out that way. It might have continued thus: 13 Q — B 4, B — Kt 2; 14 Q × B P, B × P; 15 Kt × B, Q × Kt; 16 O — O — O with considerable advantage of position for White. The text move might be considered a mild form of suicide.

13.	P × P	B — B 4
14.	Q — K B 4	B × B
15.	O — O — O	B — Kt 2
16.	R × B	Q — K 2
17.	Q — B 4	

In order to keep the Black Queen from coming into the game.

17.	....	Q R — Q 1
18.	K R — Q 1	

A better plan would have been to play R — K 1, threatening P — K 6.

18.	....	R × R
19.	R × R	R — K 1
20.	P — B 3	P — Q B 3

Of course if B × P; Kt × B, Q × Kt; R — K 3. Black with a Pawn minus fights very hard.

21.	R — K 3

The Pawn had now to be defended after Black's last move, because after B × P; Kt × B, Q × Kt;

R — K 3, Black could now play Q — Kt 1 defending the Rook.

21.	....	P — Q B 4
22.	K — B 2	P — Kt 3
23.	P — R 4	

White's plan now is to *fix* the Queen's side in order to be able to manœuvre freely on the other side, where he has the advantage of material.

23.	....	Q — Q 2
24.	R — Q 3	Q — B 1
25.	Q — K 4	Q — K 3
26.	R — Q 5	K — B 1
27.	P — B 4	K — Kt 1

Black sees that he now stands in his best defensive position, and therefore waits for White to show how he intends to break through. He notices, of course, that the White Knight is in the way of the K B P, which cannot advance to K B 4 to defend, or support rather, the Pawn at K 5.

28.	P — Q Kt 3	K — B 1
29.	K — Q 3	K — Kt 1
30.	R — Q 6	Q — B 1
31.	R — Q 5	Q — K 3
32.	P — K Kt 4	K — B 1
33.	Q — B 4	K — Kt 1
34.	Q — K 4	K — B 1

Black persists in waiting for developments. He sees that if P — K R 5, P × P; P × P, the Queen goes to R 6, and White will have to face serious difficulties. In this situation White decides that the only course is to bring his King to K Kt 3, so as to defend the squares K R 3 and K Kt 4, where the Black Queen might otherwise become a source of annoyance.

35.	K — K 2	K — Kt 1
36.	K — B 1	K — B 1
37.	K — Kt 2	K — Kt 1
38.	K — Kt 3	K — B 1

Now that he has completed his march with the King, White is ready to advance.

39. P — K R 5   P × P

39...P — K Kt 4 would be answered by Q — B 5, with a winning game.

40. P × P   Q — K 2

Against K — Kt 1; White would play Q — Kt 4, practically forcing the exchange of Queens, after which White would have little trouble in winning the ending, since Black's Bishop could not do much damage in the resulting position.

41. Q — B 5   K — Kt 1

Black overlooks the force of 42 R — Q 7. His best defence was R — Q 1; against which White could either advance the King or play Kt — R 4, threatening Kt — Kt 6 ch.

42. R — Q 7   B × P ch

This loses a piece, but Black's position was altogether hopeless.

43.	K — Kt 4	Q — B 3
44.	Kt × B	Q — Kt 2 ch
45.	K — B 4	Resigns.

The interest of this game centres mainly on the opening and on the march of the White King during the final stage of the game. It is an instance of the King becoming a fighting piece, even while the Queens are still on the board.

GAME 13. RUY LOPEZ

(New York, 1918)

White: J. S. Morrison.   Black: J. R. Capablanca.

1.	P — K 4	P — K 4
2.	Kt — K B 3	Kt — Q B 3
3.	B — Kt 5	P — Q 3
4.	Kt — B 3	B — Q 2
5.	P — Q 4	P × P
6.	Kt × P	P — K Kt 3

In this form of defence of the Ruy Lopez the development of the K B via Kt 2 is, I think, of great importance. The Bishop at Kt 2 exerts great pressure along the long diagonal. At the same time the position of the Bishop and Pawns in front of the King, once it is Castled, is one of great defensive strength. Therefore, in this form of development, the Bishop,

we might say, exerts its maximum strength   (Compare
this note with the one in the Capablanca-Burn game
at San Sebastian, page 197.)

7.	Kt — B 3	B — Kt 2
8.	B — Kt 5	Kt — B 3

Of course not K Kt — K 2 ; because of Kt — Q 5.
The alternative would have been P — B 3 ; to be
followed by K Kt — K 2 ; but in this position it is
preferable to have the Kt at K B 3.

9.	Q — Q 2	P — K R 3
10.	B — K R 4	

An error of judgment. White wants to keep the
Knight pinned, but it was more important to prevent
Black from Castling immediately. B — K B 4 would
have done this.

10.	....	O — O
11.	O — O — O	

Bold play, but again faulty judgment, unless he intended to play to win or lose, throwing safety to
the winds. The Black Bishop at Kt 2 becomes a
very powerful attacking piece. The strategical dis-
position of the Black pieces is now far superior to
White's, therefore it will be Black who will take the
offensive.

11.	....	R — K 1
12.	K R — K 1	

White wanted to keep his Q R on the open file, and consequently brings over his other Rook to the centre to defend his K P, which Black threatened to win by P — K Kt 4, followed by Kt × P.

12. .... P — Kt 4 !

Now that the K R is in the centre, Black can safely advance, since, in order to attack on the King's side, White would have to shift his Rooks, which he cannot do so long as Black keeps up the pressure in the centre.

13. B — Kt 3 Kt — K R 4

Uncovering the Bishop, which now acts along the long diagonal, and at the same time preventing P — K 5, which would be answered by Kt × B; P × Kt, Kt × P; etc., winning a Pawn.

14. Kt — Q 5 P — R 3

Black drives the Bishop away so as to *unpin* his pieces and be able to manœuvre freely.

15. B — Q 3   B — K 3

Preparing the onslaught. Black's pieces begin to beat against the King's position.

16. P — B 3

With the last move White not only blocks the action of Black's K B, but he also aims at placing his Bishop at Q Kt 1 and his Queen at Q B 2, and then advancing his K P, to check at K R 7.

16. ....   P — B 4 !

Initiating an attack to which there is no reply, and which has for its ultimate object either the winning of the White Q B or cutting it off from the game. (Compare this game with the Winter-Capablanca game at Hastings.)

17. P — K R 4   P — B 5

The Bishop is now out of action. White naturally counter attacks violently against the seemingly exposed position of the Black King, and, with **very good judgment,** even offers the Bishop.

18. P × P !   P × P !

Taking the Bishop would be dangerous, if not actually bad, while the text move accomplishes Black's object, which is to put the Bishop out of action.

19. R — R 1   B — B 2
20. K — Kt 1

This move unquestionably loses time. Since he would have to retire his Bishop to R 2 sooner or later, he might have done it immediately. It is doubtful, however, if at this stage of the game it would be possible for White to save the game.

20. ....   Kt — K 4
21. Kt × Kt   R × Kt

It was difficult to decide which way to retake. I

took with the Rook in order to have it prepared for a possible attack against the King.

22. B — R 2   Kt — B 3

Now that the White Bishop has been driven back, Black wants to get rid of White's strongly posted Knight at Q 5, which blocks the attack of the Bishop at B 2. It may be said that the Knight at Q 5 is the key to White's defence.

23. P — K Kt 3

White strives not only to have play for his Bishop, but also he wants to break up Black's Pawns in order to counter-attack. The alternative would have been 23 Kt × Kt ch, Q × Kt; and Black would be threatening R — R 4, and also Q — K 3. The student should notice that Black's drawback in all this is the fact that he is playing minus the services of his Q R. It is this fact that makes it possible for White to hold out longer.

23.	....	Kt × P
24.	B × Kt	R × B
25.	P × P	P — B 3

26. Kt — K 3

Kt — Kt 4 was the alternative, but in any event White could not resist the attack. I leave it to the reader to work this out for himself, as the variations are so numerous that they would take up too much space.

26.	....	Q — R 4
27.	P — B 4	Q × Q
28.	R × Q	P × P
29.	Kt — Kt 4	B — Kt 3

This forces the King to the corner, where he will be in a mating net.

30.	K — R 1	Q R — K 1

Now at last the Q R enters into the game and soon the battle is over.

31.	P — R 3	

If R × P, R — K 8 ch; R — Q 1, R (K 1) — K 7.

31.	....	R — K 8 ch
32.	R × R	R × R ch
33.	K — R 2	B — B 2
34.	K — Kt 3	P — Q 4

the quickest way to finish the game.

35.	B × P	P × P ch
36.	K — Kt 4	P — B 6
37.	P × P	R — K 5 ch
38.	P — B 4	R × P ch
39.	K — R 5	R × B
40.	R — Q 8 ch	K — R 2
41.	R — Q 7	B — K 3
	Resigns.	

A very lively game.

GAME 14.   QUEEN'S GAMBIT DECLINED
(New York, 1918)

White: F. J. Marshall.   Black: J. R. Capablanca.

1.	P — Q 4	P — Q 4
2.	Kt — K B 3	Kt — K B 3
3.	P — B 4	P — K 3
4.	Kt — B 3	Q Kt — Q 2
5.	B — Kt 5	B — K 2
6.	P — K 3	O — O
7.	R — B 1	P — B 3

This is one of the oldest systems of defence against the Queen's Gambit. I had played it before in this Tournament against Kostic, and no doubt Marshall expected it. At times I change my defences, or rather systems of defence; on the other hand, during a Tournament, if one of them has given me good results, I generally play it all the time.

8.	Q — B 2	P × P
9.	B × P	Kt — Q 4
10.	B × B	Q × B
11.	O — O	Kt × Kt
12.	Q × Kt	P — Q Kt 3

This is the key to this system of defence. Having simplified the game considerably by a series of exchanges, Black will now develop his Q B along the long diagonal without having created any apparent weakness. The proper development of the Q B is Black's greatest problem in the Queen's Gambit.

13.	P — K 4	B — Kt 2
14.	K R — K 1	K R — Q 1

The developing stage can now be said to be complete on both sides. The opening is over and the middle-game begins. White, as is generally the case, has obtained the centre. Black, on the other hand, is entrenched in his first three ranks, and if given time will post his Q R at Q B 1 and his Knight at K B 3, and finally play P — Q B 4, in order to break up White's centre and give full action to the Black Bishop posted at Q Kt 2. In this game White attempts to anticipate that plan by initiating an advance on the centre, which, when carefully analysed, is truly an attack against Black's K P.

15. P — Q 5   Kt — B 4!

Against Kostic in a previous game I had played Kt — B 1. It was carelessness on my part, but Marshall believed differently, otherwise he would not have played this variation, since, had he analysed this move, he would, I think, have realised that Black would obtain an excellent game.   Black now threatens not only B P × P; but also Kt × P; followed by B P × P. The position is very interesting and full of possibilities.

16.	P × K P	Kt × P (K 3)
17.	B × Kt	Q × B

played under the impression that White had to lose time in defending his Q R P, when I could play P— Q B 4, obtaining a very superior game. But, as will be seen, my opponent had quite a little surprise for me.

18. Kt — Q 4 !

18. ....   Q — K 4 !

Of course, if 18...Q × R P; 19 R — R 1 would win the Queen. The text move is probably the only satisfactory move in the position. The obvious move would have been Q — Q 2 to defend the Q B P, and then would have come 19 Kt — B 5, P — B 3; 20 Q — K Kt 3 (threatening Q R — Q 1), K — R 1; 21 Q R — Q 1, Q — K B 2; 22 P — K R 4, with a tremendous advantage in position. The text move, on the other hand, assures Black an even game at the very least, as will soon be seen.

19.	Kt × P	Q × Q
20.	R × Q	R — Q 7
21.	R — Kt 1	

A very serious error of judgment. White is under the impression that he has the better game, because he is a Pawn ahead, but that is not so. The powerful position of the Black Rook at Q 7 fully compensates Black for the Pawn minus. Besides, the Bishop is better with Rooks than the Knight (see pages 48-56, where the relative values of the Knight and Bishop are compared), and, as already stated, with Pawns on both sides of the board the Bishop is superior because of its long range. Incidentally, this ending will demonstrate the great power of the Bishop. White's best chance was to take a draw at once, thus. 21 Kt — K 7 ch K — B 1; 22 R — B 7 R — K 1 (not B × P; because P — B 3 would give White the best of it); 23 R × B (best; not Kt — Kt 6 ch, because of B P × Kt; followed by R × K P), R × Kt; 24 R — Kt 8 ch, R — K 1; 25 R × R ch, K × R, and with proper play White will draw.

It is curious that, although a Pawn ahead, White is the one who is always in danger. It is only now, after seeing this analysis, that the value of Black's 18th move Q — K 4 can be fully appreciated.

21.	....	R — K 1

With this powerful move Black begins, against White's centre, an assault which will soon be shifted against the King itself. White is afraid to play 22 P — B 3 because of P — B 4.

      22. P — K 5   P — K Kt 4

To prevent P — B 4. The White Knight is practically pinned, because he does not dare move on account of R × K P.

      23. P — K R 4

This is a sequel to the previous move. White expects to disrupt Black's Pawns, and thus make them weak.

      23. . . . .   P × P

Though doubled and isolated this Pawn exercises enormous pressure. Black now threatens R — K 3; to be followed by R — Kt 3 and P — R 6 and R 7 at the proper time.

      24. R — K I

White cannot stand the slow death any longer.

He sees danger everywhere, and wants to avert it by giving up his Queen's side Pawns, expecting to regain his fortunes later on by taking the initiative on the King's side.

24. .... R — K 3 !

Much better than taking Pawns. This forces White to defend the Knight with the Rook at K 1, because of the threat R — Kt 3.

25. R (K 1) — Q B 1   K — Kt 2

Preparatory to R — Kt 3. The game is going to be decided on the King's side, and it is the isolated double Pawn that will supply the finishing touch.

26. P — Q Kt 4   P — Kt 4

To prevent P — Kt 5, defending the Knight and liberating the Rooks.

27. P — R 3   R — Kt 3
28. K — B 1   R — R 7

Notice the remarkable position of the pieces. White cannot move anything without incurring some loss. His best chance would have been to play 29 P — K 6, but that would only have prolonged the game, which is lost in any case.

      29. K — Kt 1   P — R 6

      30. P — Kt 3   P — Q R 3

Again forcing White to move and to lose something thereby, as all his pieces are tied up.

      31. P — K 6   R × K P

Not even now can White move the Knight because of P — R 7 ch; K × P, R — R 3 ch; K — Kt 1, R — R 8 mate.

      32. P — Kt 4   R — R 3

      33. P — B 3

If 33 P — Kt 5, P — R 7 ch; 34 K — R 1, R × Kt; 35 R × R, R × P, winning easily.

33.	....	R — Q 3
34.	Kt — K 7	R (Q 3) — Q 7
35.	Kt — B 5 ch	K — B 3
36.	Kt — R 4	K — Kt 4
37.	Kt — B 5	R — Kt 7 cb
38.	K — B 1	P — R 7
39.	P — B 4 ch	K × B P
40.	Resigns.	

An ending worth very careful study.

Finis